THE POLITICAL ROLE
OF THE
GENERAL ASSEMBLY

United Nations Studies: No. 7

CARNEGIE ENDOWMENT FOR INTERNATIONAL PEACE
405 WEST 117TH STREET
NEW YORK 27, NEW YORK

United Nations Studies

THE POLITICAL ROLE
OF THE
GENERAL ASSEMBLY

By

H. FIELD HAVILAND, JR.

Department of Political Science
Haverford College

United Nations Studies: No. 7

CARNEGIE ENDOWMENT FOR INTERNATIONAL PEACE
405 West 117th Street
New York
1951

MARSTIN PRESS
NEW YORK, N. Y.
U. S A
438

FOREWORD

By

Nasrollah Entezam

The Carnegie Endowment for International Peace has for several years published studies in connection with United Nations activities by well-known authors and college professors. These studies are a treasure house of information for scholars of international affairs who wish to keep themselves abreast of the work of the United Nations.

The present study dealing with the political role of the General Assembly was undertaken by Dr. Field Haviland of Haverford College who has conferred the distinction of writing this introduction on me. With every desire to avail myself of this privilege, my first reaction was to ask to be excused because — and I say this without any false modesty — I did not consider myself sufficiently qualified to introduce either the subject or the author to the reader.

If I did not give way to my hesitation it was mainly because of the honor my colleagues had conferred upon me and upon my country of electing me to preside at the Fifth Session of the General Assembly. As President I was in a unique position to follow the discussions and to participate in the activities of the United Nations. Consequently, I feel that I can take the liberty of trying the patience of the reader by making a few observations of a general nature.

I do not propose to say anything regarding the activities of the General Assembly, which is the subject matter of this book, because I do not wish to repeat what the author has described much better than I can; I will therefore only touch briefly on my impressions of the Fifth Session.

Foreword

The General Assembly stands out and ranks first among the organs of the United Nations because it is more representative and consequently more democratic. While the Councils are composed of representatives of a limited number of Governments, the General Assembly alone includes all member States without exception. For this very reason the Charter has given the General Assembly wide powers and recognized its right to discuss any question or any matter within the scope of the United Nations Charter.

Furthermore, the non-permanent members of the Security Council, the members of the Trusteeship Council and of the Economic and Social Council are all elected by the General Assembly which, in conjunction with the Security Council, also elects the Judges of the International Court of Justice and the Secretary-General.

The importance of the General Assembly is thus evident and the field of its activities is widening day by day. The more the Security Council — for reasons which it is unnecessary to dwell upon — encounters obstacles in carrying out its duties the more will the functions of the General Assembly be enlarged.

The resolution entitled "United Action for Peace," details of which are described in this book, is evidence of this. In stating, on the occasion of its adoption, that it was the most important resolution yet passed by any Assembly, I do not think I was exaggerating.

In adopting this resolution the General Assembly prepared itself to face the most critical emergencies and to furnish the means to stop or punish an aggressor when necessary.

At first it was believed that an Assembly composed of all the member States could not reach important decisions with sufficient rapidity or that the smaller Governments which do not play an important role in world affairs or which do not have obligations and responsibilities would exhibit apathy and irresponsibility in dealing with questions in which they were not directly concerned.

Experience has proved this fear to be groundless. Not only have the smaller nations shown a keen sense of responsibility; indeed at times they have prevented the General Assembly from going astray and guided it to the right track. One outstanding illustration will suffice:

Under the Treaty of Peace with Italy it had been agreed that if the question of the former Italian colonies could not be settled by the Great Powers within one year the matter should be referred to the General Assembly. As the Great Powers failed to reach an agreement on that question it was referred to the General Assembly. In the spring of 1949 the majority of the members felt that the time was still not ripe for the independence of Libya and prepared a resolution to place that territory under the trusteeship system. At the plenary meeting an unexpected change in the vote of a very small nation prevented the requisite two-thirds majority from being obtained. Subsequently, in the autumn of the same year, independence was promised to Libya. The representative of Haiti, who proved how important the role of a small nation can be and how one vote can affect the destiny of a country, deserves the highest eulogy for the independence and judgment he displayed on that occasion.

The Fifth General Assembly, which has been one of the longest and which is still in session, began its labors at a most critical moment and passed through many anxious months.

The war in Korea took up most of our time and thoughts. This being the first time that an international organization had replied to force by force, the world awaited the outcome of this test with great anxiety.

Fortunately, as I write these lines, discussions for a truce are under way and if these negotiations bear fruit and peace is established in the war-torn country of Korea and if the resolution, "United Action for Peace," is implemented the designation of "The Assembly of Collective Security" given to the Fifth Session will be most appropriate.

If I express an ardent hope that the next Assembly in Paris will follow through the work started in this Session, to provide the General Assembly with a Police Force against would-be aggressors, it is because of a sincere belief that its existence will deter aggression and make the actual employment of such a Force never necessary.

Washington, D.C.

July 14, 1951

TABLE OF CONTENTS

INTRODUCTION

On 3 November 1950, the General Assembly of the United Nations adopted what *The New York Times* described as:

a history-making resolution under which members of the United Nations could be requested by the Assembly to provide armed forces against aggression if the veto prevented the Security Council from taking action. ... Nasrollah Entezam, President of the Assembly, said after announcing the vote that it was the most important resolution adopted by any Assembly.[1]

Thus the public's attention was drawn dramatically to the "Uniting for Peace" resolution, the latest manifestation of an important change that has been taking place within the United Nations during the last five years. In response to various political forces the General Assembly has assumed ever-increasing authority with respect to so-called "political" issues, as compared with the Security Council, which was originally expected to be the dominant organ in the political field.

The intense heat that has been generated by this development is indicated by two conflicting utterances made at the end of the debate which produced the resolution cited above. John Foster Dulles of the United States delegation declared:

We must organize dependably the collective will to resist aggression. If the Security Council does not do so, then this Assembly must do what it can by invoking its residual power of recommendation.[2]

Andrei Vyshinsky of the Soviet Union replied:

If there is no agreement between the great Powers on fundamental matters affecting the organization of international relations, then whether the General Assembly decides these questions

---

[1] *The New York Times*, 4 November 1950, p. 1.
[2] Official Records of the Fifth Session of the General Assembly, Plenary Meetings, Verbatim Record, p. 294.

without the veto or whether the Security Council decides them
with the veto, there will still be a threat to peace....

[The new] proposals ... would destroy the Charter and obstruct
the Security Council ... and make it possible to carry on that
struggle exclusively through the General Assembly where you
have a majority ....[3]

In order to understand this crucial development it is
essential that one examine the forces that have influenced it,
the parallelism between this phenomenon and certain events
that took place under the League of Nations, the complex
forms which the change has taken, and the significant implications which stem from it. This study will examine these
several aspects in an effort both to understand this evolution
and to discover what positive recommendations may be made
regarding its future direction.

The term "political" as used in this report is a rather
slippery concept to wrestle with. Nevertheless it seems to be
generally understood in connection with United Nations
affairs to designate those questions that are so highly charged
that they are a potential threat to international peace. In
the General Assembly such matters have customarily been
assigned to the First Committee or an *Ad Hoc* Political
Committee, and it is the items dealt with by those bodies
that will hold the center of the stage in this analysis.

There is of course no clear division between "political"
and "non-political" matters as to substance. The Second
(Economic and Financial), Third (Social, Humanitarian,
and Cultural), Fourth (Trusteeship), and Sixth (Legal)
Committees are all dealing with matters that are potentially
inflammable. When the temperature of one or several of
these issues rises to a dangerous level in a particular area,
the situation is usually regarded as "political" and is given
special attention.

The first major section of this analysis examines the
embryonic phase when the Assembly's role in relation to
political issues was being created at Dumbarton Oaks and

---

[3] *Ibid.*, pp. 329, 334.

San Francisco. Three principal elements are singled out for special treatment:

(1) the Assembly's authority to deal with specific questions that affect only a limited sector of the world community, such as disputes among two or more nations;

(2) the authority to deal with general political problems that affect the great majority of countries, such as resolutions on armaments regulation and methods of pacific settlement; and

(3) the organizational structure which was created to implement the first two mandates.

The second section analyzes the political role of the Assembly in action: its consideration during the first five years of its existence of 22 major issues, involving approximately 150 separate resolutions, which are divided for the purposes of this analysis into the three categories just mentioned. A list of these issues and the resolutions adopted to deal with them appears in the Appendix of this study.

It should be made clear at the outset that this is not a mere X-ray photograph of an inanimate mechanism. No institution can be understood apart from the interest groups that shape it. An institution is not buildings, tables and chairs but those very interests themselves acting collectively for certain specified purposes. This is an obvious fact that is frequently overlooked by people who talk about the Assembly as if it had an existence separate from the activities of its members. It is also forgotten by those who think of the Charter as having a fixed and immutable meaning quite independent of the varying interpretations which different nations have applied to the document since it was first formulated.

At the same time it would be quite incorrect to think that the members of the Assembly have retained just as much freedom of action as they had before it was created. It is not merely a meeting place. Its activities are constant evidence that each member has agreed to yield some degree of freedom in order to work with other nations according to certain accepted patterns of procedure. The Assembly is in fact nothing more nor less than its members working together within the framework of those patterns of procedure. The real and significant impact of this arrangement upon international relations is indicated by the fact that states as powerful as the United States and the Soviet Union find a positive advantage, in terms of their own national interests, in participating regularly in the Assembly's operations.

As Charles Easton Rothwell has put it:

The very existence of international organizations . . . has injected a new force into the world community and has altered the configurations of world politics. Regardless of the fact that the states which created international organizations have usually intended that they should remain simply instruments for internation collaboration, they have inevitably become something more.

The organizations have been able to exert such influence because . . . they have served as institutions through which contending political forces can be brought continuously face to face in a regularized manner.[4]

---

[4] Charles Easton Rothwell, "International Organization and World Politics," *International Organization*, Vol. III, No. 4 (November, 1949), pp. 612, 615.

I. THE ASSEMBLY'S POLITICAL ROLE — IN EMBRYO

In attempting to understand the operations of any organization one should strive to be constantly aware of two dimensions that are extremely important and at the same time extremely difficult for any solitary observer at a single moment in the march of events to comprehend. The first dimension is that of historical continuity; the second, the interrelatedness of the many strands in any cross-section of human experience. Thus the creation and development of the General Assembly's authority in the political field can be understood only in terms of various continuous and inter-related factors.

BACKGROUND OF THE CHARTER

Great Power Views

Undoubtedly the major elements that determined from the very beginning the character of the General Assembly's mandate in the political sphere were the views of the great powers, which had been conditioned not only by the immediate events of World War II but also by the experience of the past, particularly the interwar years. Of those powers there seems to be general agreement that the United States was the dominant factor in planning the United Nations to an even greater extent than it had been in 1919 in connection with the League of Nations.[1] The fundamental goal of

---

[1] For a detailed account of the planning stage, see *The Memoirs of Cordell Hull* (New York, Macmillan, 1948), especially Vol. II, Part 8; Eugene P. Chase, *The United Nations in Action* (New York, McGraw-Hill, 1950), Ch. II; Vera M. Dean, *The Four Cornerstones of Peace* (New York, Whittlesey House, 1946); Leland Goodrich and Edvard Hambro, *Charter of the United Nations: Commentary and Documents* (Rev. ed., Boston, World Peace Foundation, 1949); *Postwar Foreign Policy Preparation 1939-1945*, Department of State Publication 3580, General Foreign Policy Series 15 (Washington, 1949); and Sumner Welles, *Where Are We Heading?* (New York and London, Harper, 1946).

the United States was to establish a collective organization capable of maintaining international peace by placing primary control over security questions in the hands of the great powers. A secondary goal was to begin about where the League left off in the promotion of various economic and social programs which many thought had been the most constructive contributions made by the League. Nevertheless, as Vera M. Dean commented in 1946, the general impression in the minds of many who helped to construct the new organization was that the "core" of the United Nations was to be a "coalition of the great powers, victors in World War II, who assume responsibility for the maintenance of world security and claim authority sufficient to discharge this responsibility."[2] The historical continuity of this idea is obvious enough, running back through the League Council, the Concert of Europe and beyond.

During the early planning stages of 1942 and 1943 President Roosevelt, influenced particularly by Prime Minister Churchill and Under Secretary of State Sumner Welles, emphasized the potential role of regional organizations that would have primary responsibility for the maintenance of peace in their respective bailiwicks. Above these groups would be a supreme universal council with final authority to deal with security matters that could not be settled at the lower level. The council would be composed of seven states representing the regional systems plus the four great powers: the United States, the Soviet Union, the United Kingdom and China: "the major powers possessing the armed force required to keep the peace would necessarily have to be given all the authority needed to act when action was indispensable to avert war."[3] Above all, President Roosevelt was haunted by one overriding concern: that "We won't get any strong international organization unless we can find the way by which the Soviet Union and the United States can work together to build it up as the years go by."[4] He

---

2 *Op. cit.*, p. 67.
3 Welles, *op. cit.*, p. 24.
4 *Ibid.*, pp. 29-30.

never felt that a world assembly could or should play a significant role in security affairs.

Secretary of State Cordell Hull, on the other hand, felt that there was a "basic cleavage" between the President's views and his own, which placed more emphasis on the over-all "general international organization," the wording used in the Moscow Declaration of October 1943.[5] Nothing was said in that statement about regional security organizations against which Secretary Hull argued strongly at Moscow. By April 1944 the Department of State had prepared a draft plan which gave both the proposed general assembly and executive council approximately the same authority in the non-military political field. At the same time the council was to have "primary responsibility for the maintenance of international security and peace" and was to be the sole organ to commit the United Nations to the use of collective force. The specific powers assigned to the assembly by the April draft were:

a. to make . . . reports on and recommendations for the peaceful adjustment of any situation or controversy the continuation of which it deems likely to impair the general welfare;

b. to assist the executive council . . . in enlisting the cooperation of all states . . . with respect to: . . .

(1) the settlement of a dispute . . . ;

(2) the maintenance or restoration of peace, and

(3) any other matters within the jurisdiction of the Council . . . .[6]

By July 1944 the United States had also added to its plan a proposal for an economic and social program to be administered under a special council responsible to the assembly. This project was largely shaped by the thinking current in the last years of the League, especially as reflected in the Bruce Report of 1939.[7] Other suggestions anticipated a strengthening of the League Mandates System.

---

[5] Hull, *op. cit.,* pp. 1642-43.

[6] *Postwar Foreign Policy Preparation 1939-1945,* p. 584.

[7] Martin Hill, *The Economic and Financial Organization of the League of Nations* (Washington, Carnegie Endowment for International Peace, 1946), pp. 116-19.

It was this general framework which was presented to the USSR, the United Kingdom and China during the Dumbarton Oaks Conference, August to October 1944, and was for the most part accepted by that Conference with surprisingly few changes. Only the trusteeship proposals were omitted at Dumbarton Oaks because "the Joint Chiefs [of Staff] felt that a discussion of the trusteeship system would inevitably embrace concrete questions of who should be trustee over what territories, and that dissension might therefore arise among the major Allies."[8]

The Soviet Union, according to the views it expressed before and during the Dumbarton Oaks Conference, strongly supported the United States emphasis on the importance of unity among the great powers in the maintenance of international peace, but was exceedingly reluctant to accept the United States thesis of an assembly which would be given significant political responsibilities. The Russian proposal which particularly disturbed the other powers was the suggestion that all sixteen of the Soviet Republics be granted separate votes in the organization, something which the others adamantly refused to accept. The Russians also wanted the economic and social program to be entirely separate from the political organization rather than, as the United States urged, under a special council responsible to the assembly.

In general, however, the most severe disputes arose over the organization and voting procedures of the Security Council rather than the Assembly. As one might expect, the British views were very similar to those of the United States although they, like the Russians, began by favoring a weak assembly. The attention of all three major powers, however, was focused primarily on the Council which they were determined to make the principal center of influence in the political field.

---

8 Hull, *op. cit.*, p. 1706.

Smaller Power Views

A second major force that shaped the Assembly's authority in the political sphere was the attitude of the smaller nations, particularly the important "middle" powers. The fact that they had not been invited to the Dumbarton Oaks Conference and that the proposals emerging from that Conference seemed to them to smack of excessive great power dominance were elements that contributed to their firm determination to strengthen their own influence, especially by reinforcing the role of the General Assembly. One expression of this point of view was Resolution 30 of the Inter-American Conference of February and March 1945, which called attention to

the desirability of amplifying...the powers of the General Assembly in order that its action, as the fully representative organ of the international community, may be rendered effective, harmonizing the powers of the Security Council with such amplification.[9]

Yet the smaller states, with few exceptions, did not ask that the total powers to be given the new organization be made any stronger; most of them were not advocates of world government. What they did want was a larger relative share of the power within the organization. The great powers on the other hand, intent on preserving their united front, were reluctant to consider any far-reaching amendments.

League Experience

The third important factor that contributed to the character of the new assembly's political authority was the experience of the League and its Assembly. As the United Nations was being created there was general reluctance to recognize the influence of that experience, largely because

---

[9] *Report of the Delegation of the United States of America to the Inter-American Conference on Problems of War and Peace*, Department of State Publication 2497, Conference Series 85 (Washington, 1946), Appendix L, pp. 103-04.

neither the United States nor the Soviet Union had demonstrated any great fondness for the League. Nevertheless, as Leland Goodrich pointed out in 1947,

it should be a cause neither of surprise nor of concern to find that the United Nations is for all practical purposes a continuation of the League of Nations. Rather it would be disturbing if the architects of world organization had completely or largely thrown aside the designs and materials of the past.[10]

Dumbarton Oaks Proposals

When the proposals that had been formulated during the Dumbarton Oaks Conference were finally released to the public in October 1944, they contained the following powers for the Assembly in the political field:

(1) to consider the general principles of cooperation in the maintenance of international peace and security, including the principles governing disarmament and the regulation of armaments;

(2) to discuss any questions relating to the maintenance of international peace and security brought before it by any member or members of the Organization or by the Security Council;

(3) to make recommendations with regard to any such principles or questions. Any such questions on which action is necessary should be referred to the Security Council by the General Assembly either before or after discussion. The General Assembly should not on its own initiative make recommendations on any matter relating to the maintenance of international peace and security which is being dealt with by the Security Council.

(4) to admit new members to the Organization upon recommendation of the Security Council. . . .

(5) [to] initiate studies and make recommendations for the purpose of promoting international cooperation in political, economic and social fields and of adjusting situations likely to impair the general welfare.[11]

---

[10] Leland M. Goodrich, "From League of Nations to United Nations," *International Organization,* Vol. I, No. 1 (February, 1947) , p. 20.

[11] *Proposals for the Establishment of a General International Organization,* submitted by the Dumbarton Oaks Conference, Washington, 9 October 1944, Chapter V, Section B.

These provisions represented an important grant of authority in the political field and indicate that the line between the Council and the Assembly was by no means as sharply drawn as many commentators have assumed. At the same time these passages must be read in the context of other Dumbarton Oaks provisions that still emphasized the primary responsibility of the Council for the maintenance of peace and security. By this time it was clear that in some areas such as economic and social affairs the Assembly was to be supreme; in the exercise of force under the United Nations the Security Council was to be supreme; while in other political matters, including pacific settlement, the authorities of the two organs would overlap.

FUNCTIONS OF THE GENERAL ASSEMBLY

Broad Role—Article 10

During the San Francisco Conference, which convened in April 1945, many of the smaller states, as well as certain groups within the larger states, launched a determined effort to develop and expand the Dumbarton Oaks Proposals in order to strengthen the role of the Assembly in the political field. A major symbol of that struggle and of the partial victory that was won is Article 10 of the Charter:

The General Assembly may discuss any questions or any matters within the scope of the present Charter or relating to the powers and functions of any organs provided for in the present Charter, and, except as provided in Article 12, may make recommendations to the Members of the United Nations or to the Security Council or to both on any such questions or matters.

Article 10 grew directly out of specific amendments made by twenty smaller states to give the Assembly approximately the same broad jurisdiction that the League Assembly had been given by the Covenant, *i.e.,* to "deal ... with any matter within the sphere of action of the League or affecting the peace of the world."[12] The proposal that received the

---

[12] Article 3 (3).

strongest support was suggested by Peter Fraser of New
Zealand, firmly backed by Herbert V. Evatt of Australia and
Padillo Nervo of Mexico: that the Assembly "have the right
to consider any matter within the sphere of international
relations."[13]

The Soviet Union took the most extreme opposing position, arguing that the General Assembly should not have the
right to deal with a question until the actions of an offending state

> create a situation which represents a menace to international
> peace and security. Until then, a state member is free to act not
> only in the field of its domestic policy but in the field of inter-
> national policy as well.[14]

While the United States and the United Kingdom fully
supported the protective concept of a state's "domestic jurisdiction," they never accepted the extreme USSR point of
view, which would have seriously hobbled the Assembly and
was far more restrictive than the provisions of the Dumbarton Oaks Proposals. The United States finally decided to
support the smaller powers in this matter. As John Foster
Dulles recently told the story:

> ... Secretary Stettinius took a strong line, with the unanimous
> backing of his Delegation. On June 19th he notified the Soviet
> delegates and Ambassador Harriman at Moscow that unless a
> satisfactory solution was found by noon of the next day the
> United States would propose that the conference vote its own
> text, leaving the Soviet Union to withdraw if it wanted. Precisely
> at twelve o'clock the next day, June 20th, Mr. Gromyko tele-
> phoned that he had received instructions from Moscow to concur
> in a formula that was acceptable to the conference as a whole.[15]

Article 10 was the formula. When one studies the text it
becomes clear that it actually added very little, as far as the

13 Documents of the United Nations Conference on International Organization, San Francisco, 1945 (New York and London, United Nations Information Organizations, 1945) [subsequently referred to as UNCIO, Documents],
III, p. 487.

14 *Ibid.*, V, p. 265.

15 *War or Peace* (New York, Macmillan, 1950), p. 38.

letter of the Charter is concerned, that was not already implied in the Dumbarton Oaks provisions quoted above which were incorporated in Articles 11, 13 and 14 with relatively few changes. After all, what could be broader than the Dumbarton Oaks mandate to the Assembly to "initiate studies and make recommendations for the purpose of promoting international cooperation ... and of adjusting situations likely to impair the general welfare"? The really significant contribution of Article 10 was the change it wrought in the spirit of the Dumbarton Oaks plan, proclaiming explicitly that the boundaries of the Assembly's authority to discuss and recommend should be as extensive as those of the entire Charter. Mr. Evatt hailed this victory, in which he played a major role, as "one of the most important achievements of the San Francisco Conference and one of the main democratic safeguards of the United Nations Organization."[16]

Authority to Deal With Specific Questions

Within the broad expanse of authority staked out by Article 10 the Assembly has been given certain particular mandates, one of which is to deal with disputes or questions affecting a specific sector, rather than the totality, of the international community. Article 10 itself was formulated, as Mr. Evatt has pointed out, primarily to make certain that the Assembly might consider specific political questions without being limited to the discussion of mere "general principles" or only those matters which actually involved the "maintenance of international peace and security."[17] Mr. Evatt does not seem to have noticed, however, that the Dumbarton Oaks Proposals authorized Assembly discussions and recommendations on "questions," as well as "general principles," and "situations likely to impair the general welfare," as well as "questions relating to the maintenance

---

16 Herbert V. Evatt, *The United Nations* (Cambridge, Harvard University Press, 1948), p. 20.
17 *Ibid.*, p. 19.

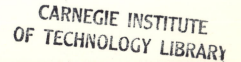

of international peace and security." As a matter of fact it is the language of the Dumbarton Oaks provisions which was incorporated with relatively few changes in what are now Articles 11 and 14 which provide the Assembly with its explicit mandate to deal with specific "questions."

In Article 11 the corresponding Dumbarton Oaks language is altered only by the addition of a provision, in keeping with Article 35 (2), authorizing non-member states to bring questions before the Assembly (Article 11 (2)) and a provision (Article 11 (3)) based upon a French suggestion authorizing the General Assembly to "call the attention of the Security Council to situations which are likely to endanger international peace and security."

The final text of Article 11 (2), as adopted by the San Francisco Conference, reads:

The General Assembly may discuss any questions relating to the maintenance of international peace and security brought before it by any Member . . . , or by the Security Council, or by a state which is not a Member . . . in accordance with Article 35, paragraph 2, and, except as provided in Article 12, may make recommendations with regard to any such questions to the state or states concerned or to the Security Council or to both. Any such question on which action is necessary shall be referred to the Security Council by the General Assembly either before or after discussion.

The last sentence of these provisions, which was taken directly from the Dumbarton Oaks draft, aroused considerable debate as to the part that the smaller states should play in connection with "action" taken by the Security Council. During this discussion the general assumption seems to have been, contrary to the views of some commentators, that "action" meant not pacific settlement but police measures under Chapter VII, especially military measures. One school of thought favored some participation by the Assembly in the Security Council's decision to engage in action,[18] but that suggestion never won any significant support. Others

---

[18] UNCIO, Documents, XII, pp. 578-79.

wanted the Assembly to have the right to review such action.[19] This led finally to the amendment of the Dumbarton Oaks provisions in order to compel the Security Council to submit to the Assembly reports on measures taken to maintain international peace and security.

The Soviet Union, however, made a major issue of its insistence that, while the Assembly might adopt a resolution on the substance of a Council report, it must have no authority to approve or disapprove the report itself since that would place the Assembly in a superior position. Neither the United States nor the United Kingdom felt strongly on the matter, since they felt it to be generally understood that the Assembly could not issue binding commands to the Council but merely recommendations. Thus they supported the Russian position. The final compromise was incorporated in Article 15:

1. The General Assembly shall receive and consider annual and special reports from the Security Council; these reports shall include an account of the measures that the Security Council has decided upon or taken to maintain international peace and security.[20]

Another provision to safeguard the interests of the smaller states resulted from a Canadian suggestion "that provision be made for the participation in decisions of the Security Council of Members not represented on it, whenever such Members are desired to take serious enforcement action."[21] At first the United States, the Soviet Union and the other sponsoring powers opposed this suggestion. Senator Vandenberg explained that the "Council would be a representative body of the Assembly, just as the Assembly would be representative of the various countries"; yet the Assembly should not "encroach" on the Council since "it was inconceivable that any action of the Council would be contrary to the

---

19 *Ibid.,* p. 297.
20 For the discussions at San Francisco, see UNCIO, Documents, IX, pp. 88, 93-94, 435, 438-39.
21 *Ibid.,* XII, p. 297.

wishes of a majority of the Assembly."[22] The Soviet Union simply argued that the Security Council must be strong and unfettered. The French and others, however, decided to support the Canadian proposal which was eventually adopted in the form of the present Article 44:

When the Security Council has decided to use force it shall, before calling upon a Member not represented on it to provide armed forces in fulfillment of the obligations assumed under Article 43, invite that Member, if the Member so desires, to participate in the decisions of the Security Council concerning the employment of contingents of that Member's armed forces.

This concession to the smaller powers noticeably reduced their insistence that the Assembly be given some control over the Council's resorting to action.

Regarding controversial Article 12, Mr. Evatt led another revolt by insisting that the Assembly should be barred from making a recommendation on a matter only so long as the "Security Council is exercising the functions assigned to it" with respect to that matter, rather than according to the Dumbarton Oaks wording, which was thought to imply that the Council might block Assembly recommendations merely by keeping matters on its agenda.[23] Mr. Evatt also wanted the Assembly to be able to decide for itself when the Security Council was actually "exercising the functions assigned to it." Altogether fourteen countries, including France, submitted amendments along these general lines. Finally Senator Vandenberg announced a compromise draft that accepted much of the Australian thesis as the basis for Article 12.

1. While the Security Council is exercising in respect of any dispute or situation the functions assigned to it in the present Charter, the General Assembly shall not make any recommendation with regard to that dispute or situation unless the Security Council so requests.

2. The Secretary-General, with the consent of the Security Council, shall notify the General Assembly at each session of

---

22 *Ibid.*, pp. 316, 296.
23 *Ibid.*, IX, p. 266.

any matters relative to the maintenance of international peace and security which are being dealt with by the Security Council and shall similarly notify the General Assembly, or the Members of the United Nations if the General Assembly is not in session, immediately the Security Council ceases to deal with such matters.

The words at the beginning of the second paragraph, "with the consent of the Security Council," seemed to indicate, contrary to the views of Mr. Evatt and others, that the Security Council, rather than the Assembly, was to be the final authority in deciding what matters were no longer being dealt with by the Council.

The last major battle regarding the Assembly's authority to deal with specific situations was fought around the standard of the "Vandenberg Amendment." In this case the initiative in strengthening the Assembly's role came from a representative of one of the great powers. Although the Dumbarton Oaks draft had provided that the Assembly might "initiate studies and make recommendations for the purpose of promoting international cooperation in [the] political . . . field . . . and of adjusting situations likely to impair the general welfare," Senator Vandenberg, in close collaboration with such advisers as John Foster Dulles, wanted to add a provision, similar to Article 19 of the League Covenant, that would authorize the Assembly to make recommendations regarding various forms of peaceful change including the revision of treaties. When this proposal was first suggested to the other sponsoring powers, Mr. Molotov of the Soviet Union firmly opposed it as a potential threat to the stability of the postwar treaties which were about to be negotiated.[24]

The compromise which seems to have paved the way for the provisions which finally became Article 14 was two-fold. First, it was understood that Chapter XII, paragraph 2, of the Dumbarton Oaks draft, later to become Article 107 of the Charter, would protect any World War II peace treaties

24 *The New York Times,* 4 May 1945, p. 12.

from Assembly intervention. Second, there was to be no specific mention in the Vandenberg Amendment of treaty revision but rather the adjustment of any situation "regardless of origin" which might impair the general welfare "or friendly relations among nations, including situations resulting from a violation of the Purposes and Principles set forth in ... [the] Charter."[25] Thus the final text of Article 14 of the Charter, as adopted by the Conference, reads:

Subject to the provisions of Article 12, the General Assembly may recommend measures for the peaceful adjustment of any situation, regardless of origin, which it deems likely to impair the general welfare or friendly relations among nations, including situations resulting from a violation of the provisions of the present Charter setting forth the Purposes and Principles of the United Nations.

It is interesting to note that, in interpreting these provisions to the Conference, Senator Vandenberg stated explicitly that they clearly included the authority to recommend the revision of treaties. Mr. Molotov replied that such an interpretation "attacks the very basis of international law, peace, and security."[26] As for the general significance of the amendments added at San Francisco one can only say that they made more explicit the provisions which had already been adopted at Dumbarton Oaks.

Limitations

Another important passage, of a somewhat different character, that deserves attention in connection with the Assembly's authority regarding specific disputes and situations, as well as all other political matters, is not to be found in Chapter IV of the Charter but rather in Chapter I, Article 2 (7):

---

25 UNCIO, Documents, IX, pp. 21-22. For developments leading to this compromise, see *The New York Times* of 4, 7, 8, 9 May 1945.

26 UNCIO, Documents, IX, pp. 150, 138; for Vandenberg's statement, see *ibid.*, p. 127.

Nothing contained in the present Charter shall authorize the United Nations to intervene in matters which are essentially within the domestic jurisdiction of any state or shall require the Members to submit such matters to settlement under the present Charter; but this principle shall not prejudice the application of enforcement measures under Chapter VII.

At Dumbarton Oaks the British had been initially responsible for the insertion in the four-power draft of a provision, applicable only to the pacific settlement section of that draft, which stated that the United Nations should not deal with "situations or disputes arising out of matters which by international law are solely within the domestic jurisdiction of the State concerned."[27] This was similar to Article 15 (8) of the League Covenant except that the League left the decision in each case entirely to the Council, whereas the Dumbarton Oaks draft did not say who was to decide what lies within the domestic sphere.

Early in the San Francisco Conference the Congressional representatives on the United States delegation became alarmed at the attempts being made by Australia and other countries to use the United Nations as an instrument for attempting to achieve "full employment" and other economic and social reforms. As protection against this kind of effort the United States was largely instrumental in persuading the sponsoring powers to adopt the language of Article 2 (7) and to make it applicable to the entire Charter rather than merely the pacific settlement provisions. In explaining this move John Foster Dulles said that

this change ... had been caused ... by the change in the character of the Organization .... The scope ... was now broadened to include functions which would enable the Organization to eradicate the underlying causes of war as well as to deal with crises leading to war. ... This broadening of the scope of the Organization ... engendered special problems.

As provided in the amendment ... no one ... would go behind the governments in order to impose its desires. The amendment

---

[27] Chapter VIII, paragraph 7. See also, Hull, *op. cit.*, p. 1705.

recognized the distinct value of the individual social life of each state.[28]

Thus was born a provision which was potentially a far stronger barrier to international action than the corresponding Covenant provision had been. Not only did this passage apply to the whole Charter, but it barred United Nations action in matters only "essentially" rather than "solely" within domestic jurisdiction. Furthermore it neither required that the definition of domestic jurisdiction in each case be decided according to international law nor did it specify any agency as the final authority to make such decisions, thus leaving it to the parties to interpret the provision for themselves. At the same time it should be noted that some framers of the Charter believed that the omission of any reference to international law might allow a more liberal interpretation of the passage than would otherwise be possible.

Obligations to Dependent Peoples

Because today's world is breaking out all over with a persistent rash of national independence movements in many non-self-governing territories, the Assembly's role in trusteeship matters is directly related to its functions regarding specific situations and disputes. Although the trusteeship system cannot be given full attention in this report, it will be mentioned briefly as an important ancillary field. The whole development of the concept of international trusteeship with respect to dependent peoples arises out of a most interesting and most complex combination of both humanitarian and self-interested national motives.[29]

The first official commitment on the part of the great powers to a United Nations trusteeship system was agreed upon at the Yalta Conference in February 1945. Although

---

28 UNCIO, Documents, VI, pp. 507-08.

29 For early history, see M. F. Lindley, *The Acquisition and Government of Backward Territory in International Law* (London, Longmans, Green, 1926) and A. H. Snow, *The Question of Aborigines in the Law and Practice of Nations* (New York and London, G. P. Putnam, 1921).

the United States took the lead in favoring a continuation of the general League system, it had a difficult time formulating its position in preparation for the San Francisco Conference because of strong military and Congressional pressure to annex the former mandated Japanese islands in the Pacific.[30] This issue complicated United States negotiations on trusteeship throughout the Conference and was feared by some to be a possible obstacle to Senatorial approval of the Charter. In general the British and French wanted to retain control of their former mandated areas subject to no more stringent regulation than had been exercised by the League. The USSR looked upon the trusteeship problem with mixed interests. On the one hand it asked for a trusteeship in Tripolitania[31]; at the same time it urged that the system be used as a lever for granting independence to former mandated territories. China tended to side with the smaller nations, especially those that had only recently achieved self-rule, in encouraging the aspirations of all non-self-governing peoples and in urging direct United Nations administration of trust territories wherever possible.

The compromise finally reached at San Francisco provided for the *voluntary* placing of territories under the United Nations Trusteeship System and allowed either direct administration by the United Nations or administration by one or more states. Territories that might be placed under the new Trusteeship System were to include: (1) territories then held under mandate, (2) those which might be detached from World War II enemy states, and (3) those placed under the system by states currently responsible for their administration. The mandatory powers such as the United Kingdom and France, as well as the United States, insisted that the Charter state specifically that it was a

matter for subsequent agreement as to which territories in the foregoing categories will be brought under the trusteeship system

---

30 Dulles, *op. cit.,* p. 77.
31 James F. Byrnes, *Speaking Frankly* (New York and London, Harper, 1947) , pp. 95-96.

and upon what terms [and that] the terms . . . shall be agreed upon by the states directly concerned, including the mandatory power in the case of territories held under mandate by a Member of the United Nations, and shall be approved . . . [by the Trusteeship Council and the General Assembly].[32]

Some of the smaller countries, such as Egypt, opposed these provisions, insisting that full title and control over the former mandated territories should be vested in the United Nations, but they were unable to win any significant support for their views.

The United States, because of its interests in the former mandated Japanese Pacific islands, was largely responsible for including in the Charter authority to declare certain trust territories "strategic areas" to be administered under the supervision of the Security Council, where the United States was protected by the "veto," rather than under the Trusteeship Council.

The basic objectives of the Trusteeship System were to include the following:

a. to further international peace and security;
b. to promote the political, economic, social, and educational advancement of the inhabitants . . . and their progressive development towards self-government or independence . . .
c. to encourage respect for human rights and for fundamental freedoms . . . .[33]

General supervisory authority over the system was placed in the hands of a Trusteeship Council which in turn was to be responsible to the General Assembly. Because of the insistence of the Soviet Union, all of the permanent members of the Security Council are represented on the Trusteeship Council. The other members include the administering powers other than the permanent members and a sufficient number of additional non-administering powers, elected by

---

[32] Articles 77 and 79.
[33] Article 76.

the Assembly, to make the numbers of administering and non-administering countries equal.

Unlike the Permanent Mandates Commission, the Trusteeship Council is specifically authorized to prepare a questionnaire which the administering powers must answer, to send visiting missions to the trust territories, to accept petitions directly rather than through the administering states, and to administer directly territories that may be submitted for that purpose. In reviewing all of these provisions one is impressed with the fact that the general framework of the United Nations Trusteeship System is essentially that of the League Mandates System except that the Trusteeship Council is a stronger and more important body than was the Permanent Mandates Commission, especially in its authority with respect to visiting missions and the direct receipt of petitions. Moreover, in view of the growing aspirations of non-self-governing peoples throughout the world, the Assembly's functions in this field promised to become one of its most important responsibilities.

Closely linked to the United Nations Trusteeship System as set forth in Chapters XII and XIII of the Charter is Chapter XI, entitled "Declaration Regarding Non-Self-Governing Territories," which is one of the most significant innovations introduced at San Francisco. In that chapter the

Members of the United Nations which have or assume responsibilities for the administration of territories whose peoples have not yet attained a full measure of self-government recognize the principle that the interests of the inhabitants of these territories are paramount, and accept as a sacred trust the obligation to promote to the utmost within the system of international peace and security . . . , the well-being of the inhabitants of these territories, and, to this end:

a. to ensure . . . their political, economic, social, and educational advancement . . .

b. to develop self-government . . . [and]

e. to transmit regularly to the Secretary-General for information purposes . . . statistical and other information . . . relating to economic, social, and educational conditions in the territories for which they are respectively responsible. . . .

While the San Francisco Conference did not accept a Chinese proposal that the objective of "independence" be included in Chapter XI, "independence" was adopted as an alternative objective together with "self-government" under the Trusteeship System. Altogether, this Declaration embodies a far more extensive and specific pledge on the part of colonial powers regarding their international responsibilities for their non-self-governing peoples than had ever appeared in any previous commitment. Furthermore, on the foundation of this Declaration the United Nations has initiated a remarkable development which will be discussed below.

General Political Problems

For centuries men have dreamed with Tennyson of a truly international "parliament of man." Yet at San Francisco, in spite of the labors of private groups that urged world government, there was almost no official support, by either small or large nations, for granting the Assembly binding legislative powers. Above all neither the United States nor the Soviet Union would have considered such a proposal. As Vera M. Dean wrote in 1946:

Desirable as . . . a [world] federation may seem, it is precluded by the vast differences in political, economic, and social development that exist among nations, by the divergences in their policies resulting from differences in historical experience, and by their mutual doubts and suspicions which, in many cases, have been enhanced rather than alleviated by the war.[34]

Nevertheless, the delegations at San Francisco were willing to authorize the General Assembly to perform the same broad policy function that had previously been assigned to the League Assembly: to discuss and make recommendations regarding general problems, in the political as well as other spheres, that affect the entire United Nations membership. It should also be noted that in the closely related economic and social fields the Assembly's general policy function was

---

[34] *Op. cit.,* p. 22.

given far more extensive areas to roam than had ever been possible in the days of the League.

Article 10 made explicit the fact that the Assembly's jurisdiction was to extend to the uttermost boundaries of the Charter. Article 11 (1), which was taken almost *verbatim* from the Dumbarton Oaks draft, spelled out in further detail the general powers of the Assembly:

The General Assembly may consider the general principles of cooperation in the maintenance of international peace and security, including the principles governing disarmament and the regulation of armaments, and may make recommendations with regard to such principles to the Members or to the Security Council or both.

Under the provisions of both the Covenant and the Charter, responsibility for the implementation of these armament passages was assigned to the Councils under the leadership of the great military powers. However, while the Covenant placed major stress upon this problem, particularly from the point of view of disarmament, the Charter reflected a primary concern for collective security and positive economic and social programs. Both at Dumbarton Oaks and at San Francisco attention was focused more upon the "regulation" of armaments than upon outright "disarmament."

In Article 13 (la), the Assembly is authorized to initiate studies and make recommendations for the purpose of:

promoting international cooperation in the political field and encouraging the progressive development of international law and its codification. ...

At San Francisco, discussion of this provision revolved largely around the subject of the development of international law. China had taken the initiative in this matter, during the second phase of the Dumbarton Oaks Conference, by suggesting that the Assembly be empowered to consider "the development and revision of the rules and principles of international law." The other sponsoring powers accepted the concept of "development" but opposed "revision." At San Francisco the Philippines and Liberia urged that the Assembly also promote the codification of international law, a concept dearer to the hearts of Roman Law states than those that follow Common Law. The sponsoring powers finally agreed to include codification but still rejected revision. They preferred rather to speak of the "progressive development" of law, much to the annoyance of some of the smaller states, including Australia, Belgium and Mexico.[35]

The Philippines also proposed that the Assembly be given the authority "to enact rules of international law which should become binding upon members after such rules shall have been approved by the Security Council," but only the Philippines itself voted in favor of this suggestion.[36] Belgium wanted to bestow formally upon the Assembly a function which the League Assembly had performed without specific authority: to "submit general conventions for the consideration of states . . . with a view to securing their approval. . . ." The United States delegation argued that special conferences, rather than the Assembly, should do the detailed work of drafting conventions. The Soviet Union feared that the Belgian suggestion as applied to the political field would interfere with the Security Council's prerogatives. Although twenty-five delegations finally supported Belgium, the amendment failed to win a two-thirds majority.[37] Nevertheless many of the delegations insisted that Article 13, reinforced by Article 10, could be interpreted to authorize Assembly recommendations in the form of conventions,[38] an interpretation which was subsequently put into effect by the actual practice of the Assembly.

Article 14, discussed above in connection with specific questions, was intended to authorize, implicitly if not explicitly, recommendations regarding the revision of treaties. Obviously this might affect general international agreements

---

35 UNCIO, Documents, IX, pp. 177-78.
36 *Ibid.*, p. 70.
37 *Ibid.*, p. 80.
38 See *ibid.*, VIII, p. 208 for statement by Herbert V. Evatt.

as well as commitments of a more limited scope, but this Article certainly did not exceed, nor was it even as specific as, Article 19 of the Covenant.

The San Francisco planners also saw clearly that Assembly recommendations on general political problems, such as regulation of armaments and methods of pacific settlement, would necessarily be closely related to and affected by the extensive economic and social program which was provided for in Chapter IX of the Charter as the best positive means of alleviating international tensions. The basis for this program was Chapter IX of the Dumbarton Oaks draft, fashioned largely in the image of United States plans discussed above, which provided among other things that:

the Organization should facilitate solutions of international economic, social, and other humanitarian problems and promote respect for human rights and fundamental freedoms. Responsibility for the discharge of this function should be vested in the General Assembly and, under the authority of the General Assembly, in an Economic and Social Council.

At San Francisco many nations, particularly the debtor and planned-economy states, were eager to make these provisions even stronger, while the United States delegation, aware of Congressional resistance, was reluctant to go any further. A typical example of this conflict was the United States opposition to the inclusion of a specific commitment to promote "higher standards of living" and "full employment," a pledge which was finally adopted in spite of the United States protests. Other additions to the Dumbarton Oaks text, adopted largely at the insistence of the smaller powers, included raising the Economic and Social Council to the level of a principal United Nations organ and providing that:

(1) Members pledge themselves to take joint and separate action in cooperation with the Organization for the achievement of the purposes set forth in Article 55;

(2) The Economic and Social Council may ... prepare draft conventions for submission to the General Assembly, ... may

call ... international conferences on matters falling within its competence [and] ... may coordinate the activities of the specialized agencies. ...[39]

ORGANIZATION

The planners at Dumbarton Oaks, San Francisco and London were clearly aware of the fact that the effectiveness of the Assembly's political role would depend to a large extent on the organizational structure that was built to support it. Although some Assembly bodies, such as the First Committee, are more closely identified with the political sphere than others, it is important to keep in mind their relationship to the larger framework of the Assembly as a whole, which necessarily affects the way in which political problems are handled. The particular matters that will be singled out for special attention are: the Assembly's membership, its structure including certain of its committees, and its voting procedure.

Membership

On the question of membership the great powers had decided from the beginning that the United Nations should not at the outset attempt universality of membership, one reason being that certain of these powers had in mind countries that they wanted to bar from participation. The organization was to be composed of a core of "original" members consisting of those states which signed the United Nations Declaration of 1 January 1942. Gradually, with primary discretion in the hands of the permanent members of the Security Council, others would be added to that core. The only criterion stipulated in the Dumbarton Oaks draft to govern admission was that those admitted should be "peace-loving states."[40] The proposed role of the Assembly in this matter was merely to "admit new members to the organiza-

---

[39] Articles 56, 62 (3) and 63 (2) .
[40] Chapter III.

tion upon recommendation of the Security Council."[41] On the other hand many of the smaller states, especially the Latin Americans, favored the principle of immediate universality. Others, among the smaller nations which did not believe that the time was ripe for universality, wanted to limit the authority of the Security Council in this matter by giving the Assembly a stronger role and by making the criteria that were to govern the Council's decisions more specific. While some extremists wanted to eliminate the Security Council's prior authority altogether, Australia's Evatt tried to find a middle way by suggesting that the Assembly be authorized to

admit new members provided that it shall not, without the recommendation of the Security Council, admit . . . a State which at any time since September 1, 1939 has been at war with any member of the United Nations.[42]

The sponsoring powers stood firm however and defeated these proposals.

On the question of criteria the Netherlands wanted to make admission dependent upon the existence of "political institutions which insure that the state is the servant of its citizens," and "observance of the principle of *pacta sunt servanda*."[43] Australia and Norway wanted to include some mention of respect for the terms of the Charter.[44] Finally the United States and the United Kingdom worked out a compromise text incorporating the Australian and Norwegian views which became Article 4 (1):

Membership in the United Nations is open to all . . . peace-loving states which accept the obligations contained in the present Charter and, in the judgment of the Organization, are able and willing to carry out these obligations.

In view of the current discussions regarding the membership problem, it is interesting to note that the criterion regarding

---

41 Chapter V, Section B (2).
42 UNCIO, Documents, VIII, p. 290.
43 *Ibid.*, VII, p. 18.
44 *Ibid.*, p. 12.

"democratic institutions" was not included because it was thought, in the words of one sub-committee, to "imply an undue interference with internal arrangements."[45]

In general one can say regarding the membership discussions at San Francisco that, except for the few minor changes which were accepted, the great powers quelled the opposition without any serious sacrifices. Furthermore, the Assembly emerged with a weaker role in this sphere than the League Assembly, which had been given the authority to admit members by a two-thirds vote without Council concurrence. In the League the great powers had not considered it essential to their interests to have absolute control over admission to the organization.

Structure

Only the broad outlines of Assembly structure and procedure were delineated in the provisions of the Charter. Most of the details were added by the Preparatory Commission and its Executive Committee which met in London between August 1945 and January 1946, and formulated Rules of Procedure for submission to the first session of the Assembly.

As one might expect, the League Assembly served as the chief model for the provisions that were drafted. It was decided at San Francisco, with little discussion, to adopt the Dumbarton Oaks plan that the Assembly should "meet in regular annual sessions and in such special sessions as occasion may require."[46] This followed the general practice of the League although the original expectation in 1919 had been that the League Assembly would probably meet only every four years. The Charter, like the Covenant, limited the size of delegations, though the number was increased from three in the League Assembly to five in the United Nations General Assembly.[47]

---

[45] For the final decisions, see *ibid.*, pp. 36-37.
[46] Chapter V, Section D (1) ; United Nations Charter, Article 20.
[47] Article 9 (2) .

As in the case of the League, it was anticipated that the President of the Assembly would be its most important and influential officer. Another tradition was continued by providing in the Rules for the election of a number of Vice Presidents — eight in the League Assembly, seven in the General Assembly — among whom, it was understood, the five permanent members of the Security Council would always be represented. The other two Vice Presidents and the Chairmen of the standing committees would be chosen from the smaller countries. The most important committee in the political field was to be the First, or Political and Security, Committee which the Assembly President during the first special session called the "highest and broadest committee."[48] Obviously, however, this body would be directly affected in many respects by the work of the other five main committees, especially the Fourth (Trusteeship) and Sixth (Legal). Since these main committees would be composed of representatives of all United Nations Members, they would not be of very manageable proportions. Yet the absence of anything like party organizations, except for a few unofficial blocs, made it obviously impossible to try to reduce the size of these bodies. On the other hand, the establishment of more flexible bodies was authorized by Article 22 of the Charter, adopted directly from the Dumbarton Oaks text, which empowered the Assembly to set up "such subsidiary organs as it deems necessary for the performance of its functions." Since none of this basic machinery was very different from the League pattern it was accepted with relatively little disagreement.

The creation of the General Committee however aroused debate that gave clear evidence of the tensions which lay just beneath the surface. Again imitating the League, it was proposed that a General Committee be established, comprised as before of the President, Vice Presidents, and Committee Chairmen, to act as a steering group. One principal

---

[48] Official Records of the First Special Session of the General Assembly, Vol. I, Plenary Meetings, Verbatim Record, 28 April-15 May 1947, p. 26.

issue which was immediately raised by the Soviet Union was that it wanted some assurance that its bloc would be properly represented. Many of the smaller states, aware of the fact that the representation of the great powers would be heavily weighted, wanted to prohibit the Committee from making any "political" decisions. These demands were eventually satisfied by providing in the Assembly's Rules that the Vice Presidents were to be elected "on the basis of ensuring the representative character of the General Committee,"[49] that committee officers were to be elected "on the basis of equitable geographical distribution," as well as "experience and personal competence,"[50] and that the Committee might not "decide any political question."[51] The latter prohibition seemed to many to be rather superfluous since the proposed function of the Committee had never been more than to advise the Assembly regarding its agenda and the general organization of its business. In view of these various limitations and the political differences which they revealed, many observers feared that the Committee could not provide the leadership which they believed the Assembly would need.

Voting Procedure

Not only the Assembly's structure, but also its procedures were borrowed largely from the League Assembly. Perhaps the most noteworthy innovation was the decision to allow Assembly decisions on "important" matters, including the "maintenance of international peace and security," to be decided by a two-thirds majority; others, including decisions on what is an "important" matter, by a simple majority. This plan, based for the most part on the United States proposals, was adopted by the Dumbarton Oaks Conference and accepted at San Francisco as part of Article 18 with no serious disagreement and few changes. This seemed, on

---

[49] Rules of Procedure of the General Assembly, 12 December 1947, Rule 27, p. 6.
[50] *Ibid.*, Rule 94, p. 18.
[51] *Ibid.*, Rule 35, p. 7.

paper, to be a great advance in comparison with the League Covenant provision which required that, with the exception of certain specified matters, "decisions at any meeting of the Assembly [must be made with] the agreement of all the Members of the League represented at the meeting." In practice, however, the League had been able to discover many holes in that fence through the judicious acceptance of abstentions and less than unanimous decisions on *voeux,* questions of procedure, etc.[52]

The willingness of the great powers to accept two-thirds majorities rather than unanimous decisions in the Assembly is explained not only by the League Assembly's experience with the rule of unanimity, but also by the fact that they expected the plenary body to be far less important than the Security Council in the crucial political sphere limited in function as it was to the formulation of mere recommendations rather than binding commands. It is interesting to note however that legally the Council was to have no more power than the Assembly in the pacific settlement sphere under Chapter VI, *i.e.,* merely to make recommendations to the parties on methods and substance. Furthermore, a recommendation that could be made in the Council only with the unanimous consent of the permanent members could be made in the Assembly by a two-thirds majority without their consent. At the same time it was understood that a Council recommendation would exert extraordinary influence since it would be approved by all of the permanent members who might even be willing to employ collective force in the matter in accordance with Chapter VII. The smaller countries also indicated a general willingness to abandon the unanimity principle altogether without any extended discussion of the protection which they were thereby surrendering.

There was no significant support either at Dumbarton Oaks or at San Francisco for any system of weighted voting

---

[52] Margaret E. Burton, *The Assembly of the League of Nations* (Chicago, University of Chicago Press, 1941), Chapter VI.

as such, though the agreement reached at Yalta to give the Soviet Union two votes, in addition to its own vote, for the Ukrainian and the Byelorussian Republics,[53] represented a kind of weighted voting. The decision to require two-thirds rather than simple majorities on important matters was in fact a method of assuring some protection against decisions which might lack sufficient support to make them effective. It was also recognized that the views of the great powers would inevitably affect the positions of the smaller countries.

---

[53] Edward R. Stettinius, Jr., *Roosevelt and the Russians* (Garden City, Doubleday, 1949), p. 187.

II. THE ASSEMBLY'S POLITICAL ROLE — IN ACTION

On 10 January 1946, the twenty-sixth anniversary of the coming into force of the League of Nations Covenant, representatives of fifty-one countries met in the blue and gold auditorium of the Central Hall of Westminister for the first part of the first session of the United Nations General Assembly. One observer noted that, while there were many similarities between that meeting and the first meeting of the League Assembly, including the presence of Viscount Cecil and Dr. V. K. Wellington Koo, there were also certain obvious differences: less emphasis in 1946 on uncritical optimism and disarmament, more talk about security and economic and social issues, as well as more obvious tensions among the delegates, as demonstrated by the conflict between the Soviet bloc and other groups over the election of the first Assembly President.[1]

The importance of the political aspect of the Assembly's responsibilities was indicated by the first words uttered in the session by the temporary President, Dr. Eduardo Zuleta Angel of Colombia, the Chairman of the Preparatory Commission: "Determined to save succeeding generations from the scourge of war . . . we have come to this British capital . . . to constitute the General Assembly. . . ." How effective the Assembly's contribution in this respect would be, he went on to say, would "depend less on the terms of the Charter, on the functions and duties of the Assembly than on the wisdom, the judgment, the spirit of co-operation and sense of justice by which it is guided. . . ."[2]

With the opening of the first session began the five years of Assembly experience in the political field which provides

---

[1] See, for description, James Reston, in *The New York Times,* 11 January 1946, p. 1.
[2] Official Records of the First Part of the First Session of the General Assembly, Plenary Meetings, Verbatim Record, 10 January-14 February 1946, pp. 37-38.

the raw material for the analysis that follows. The tools had been created at Dumbarton Oaks, San Francisco and London. Now began the critical process of using them to deal with some of the world's most complex and explosive problems.

FIVE YEARS IN REVIEW

At the outset it is well to remind ourselves that 10 January 1946 was not an historical knife that entirely severed the cord between past and present. The Assembly in action was to be shaped by the same forces that had influenced its creation. It is also important to keep in mind the general chronological development of the Assembly from January 1946 to the present, as well as the over-all climate of international relations within which that development took place.

The first part of the first session was warmed by the glow of the World War II victory, and the Members were still relatively united as a result of the wartime alliance. Yet obvious tensions existed among the great powers, all too apparent at the Potsdam Conference held the previous summer and brought out in the open at the London meeting of the Council of Foreign Ministers in September. These centered around such issues as the peace treaties, the Balkan regimes and the occupation policies. Still the great powers maintained a united front during the beginning of the first session of the General Assembly and their agreement on the general principles of atomic energy control filled many hearts with hope. The first part of the session, intentionally limited to non-controversial organizational problems, gave rise to little friction. By the beginning of the second part, held from October to December 1946, the clouds over the Assembly had grown darker. The Paris Peace Conference in July had been noisily contentious; the Balkan elections were being severely criticized; and the Security Council had its hands full with situations involving Iran, Greece, Syria, Lebanon and Spain. In the Assembly the "Big Five" still maintained their unity on such constitutional issues as the Security Council's use of the veto and its prerogatives regarding admission to membership, but they openly opposed each other on issues such as troop information and armaments. At the same time the smaller states began to play a far more vigorous role than they had in the first part, especially in connection with the resolutions on Spain and the treatment of Indians in South Africa.

The first special session was called in the spring of 1947 at the request of the United Kingdom, which wanted the United Nations to conceive a plan that would solve the insoluble problem of Palestine. Avoiding any preliminary commitment, the Assembly initiated a thorough investigation of the matter by sending a special commission to study the situation on the spot. By the time of the second regular session in the fall of 1947, the Palestine situation was rapidly coming to a boil with open acts of violence. The general East-West rift had also deepened with the announcement in the West of the Truman Doctrine and the Marshall Plan and a declaration of defiance in the East which led to the establishment of the Cominform in October while the Assembly was in session. For the first time the United States looked frankly to the Assembly rather than to the Security Council, which had been hampered by the use of the "veto," to deal with such problems as the Balkan and Korean situations. The most significant organizational move in this direction came with the United States proposal for an interim committee to deal with political problems between Assembly sessions. A momentous Palestine partition plan was also adopted although the lack of agreement among the great powers prevented any practical decision on enforcement.

After the Assembly adjourned and it became apparent that the partition proposal would not enforce itself, the United States initiated the calling of a second special session in the spring of 1948 to consider the possibility of a trusteeship arrangement for Palestine. When the Assembly convened it defeated the United States suggestion and did no more than appoint a Mediator who was in the end, however, a surprisingly effective force in reestablishing peace. The third session convened in Paris in the fall of 1948 in an international climate of conflict that had been sharpened by the Berlin blockade, begun during the summer, and by the negotiations leading to the Atlantic Pact. During the session the Assembly approved the majority proposals of the Atomic Energy Commission; continued the efforts begun in 1947 to strengthen its activities in the political field — the Special Committee on the Balkans, the Korean Commission and the Interim Committee; and replaced the Palestine Mediator with a Conciliation Commission. During the second part of the third session, held at Lake Success in the spring of 1949, the Assembly wrestled with the disposition of the former Italian Colonies without reaching any final conclusion. It also expressed its concern regarding the alleged violation of human rights in Bulgaria and Hungary, and adopted several resolutions concerning methods of pacific settlement.

The fact that the Berlin blockade was lifted on 12 May, six days before the third session adjourned, seemed to clear the air momentarily, but the subsequent meeting of the Council of Foreign Ministers failed to solve either the German problem or any other problem. The rapid gains of the Chinese Communists also gave rise to forebodings concerning the impact of that issue upon the next session.

The Assembly surprised a great many observers, however, during the fourth session held in the fall of 1949, by succeeding in the formulation of a compromise settlement on the former Italian Colonies that was acceptable to most of the interested groups. Also adopted were measures to assist in the liquidation of the Palestine problem, to continue the Special Committee on the Balkans, the Korean Commission and the Interim Committee, and to request an advisory opinion from the International Court of Justice on the application of the peace treaties regarding the human rights violations in Bulgaria, Hungary and Rumania.

The crisis that dominated the fifth session was of course the attack on 25 June 1950 by the North Koreans upon South

Korea, which the United States persuaded the Security Council to meet with the first use of military sanctions under any international organization. To add its weight to this effort the Assembly during its fifth session adopted a resolution regarding the unification and rehabilitation of Korea and then, after the Chinese Communist intervention, formed a three-man committee to try to arrange a cease-fire. When that effort failed, the Assembly finally adopted, on 1 February 1951, a resolution condemning Communist China as an aggressor. Fearing future obstruction in the Security Council, the United States was also largely responsible for convincing the Assembly that it should prepare itself to mobilize and direct voluntary national contributions of armed contingents should the Security Council fail to take effective action. Thus the Assembly adopted the "Uniting for Peace" resolution, dramatic evidence of the rapid development of its role in the political field. Other measures included the continuation of the Balkan Committee, the acceptance of a plan to federate Eritrea with Ethiopia, the adoption of further measures regarding Palestine, and the revocation of the diplomatic sanctions recommended against Spain in 1946.

This brief chronological account indicates major landmarks along the route of this remarkable evolution of the Assembly's functions in the political sphere. Responding to a series of crises and pressures, the great majority of the Assembly's members took full advantage of the provisions of the Charter to make the plenary body a powerful force not only in pacific settlement but even in diplomatic and military coercive measures. It is against this backdrop that the following sections present a more intensive comparative analysis of the Assembly's treatment of these issues.

Interest Groups

Since the Assembly's major reason for existing is to reconcile various national interests, one can scarcely understand its operations except in terms of the interests that animate it. The fact that certain states have combined into blocs has alarmed some observers who had hoped that an international organization such as the Assembly would entirely banish the balancing of one alliance against another. Yet the coagulation of individual interests into disciplined groups in order to improve their bargaining power is an inherent part of the political process, international as well as domestic. All that an international organization can or should try to do is to limit the means and regulate the procedures by which groups seek to influence each other.

A study of the Assembly's past five years of experience indicates that few groups of nations have maintained a united front on most issues.[3] Individual states have tended rather to combine in different ways according to the various issues, with the obvious exception of the Soviet bloc which has experienced few deviations except for the recent defection of the Yugoslavs. Undoubtedly the most important issue which has divided the members has been the conflict between the East, led by the Soviet Union, and the West, led for the most part by the United States. The vote, for example, on the 1949 resolution on the "Essentials of Peace," an omnibus resolution regarding general world tensions, was 53 in favor against the 5 Soviet bloc states, with only Yugoslavia abstaining. Other issues on which the alignment has largely been based on this East-West division have included the questions of armaments regulation, the Interim Committee, Greece, Korea and the violation of human rights in Bulgaria, Hungary and Rumania. At the same time various countries have occasionally tried to take a middle position as mediators. Most recently a group of twelve Arab and Asian states have worked together to find a moderate compromise solution for the Korean conflict.

Another basis on which the members have divided has been with regard to the question of colonialism. On issues relating to trusteeship and non-self-governing territories, the anti-imperialists, including the Soviet bloc and those nations

---

3 M. Margaret Ball, "Bloc Voting in the General Assembly," *International Organization*, Vol. V, No. 1 (February, 1951), pp. 3-31.

that have at one time been subjected to colonialism, usually line up against the colonial and administering powers and their friends, primarily the United Kingdom, France, Belgium and the Netherlands, with the United States somewhere in between. Still another division is apparent in connection with the Spanish case between the anti-fascist interventionist members and the conservative non-interventionists. On the Spanish question, the Latin Americans, who might have been expected to vote in a bloc, were split into left, center and right elements.

Religion is an issue that has also divided the members. This was a factor in the Palestine partition decision with the states having large Moslem populations supporting the Arabs and those having influential Jewish and Christian populations generally backing the Israeli forces. Regarding the fourth session resolution on internationalizing Jerusalem in order to protect the holy sites, Arabs combined with Catholics to adopt the plan although a few Catholic states opposed internationalization as too extreme a method for gaining the desired end.

Finally there are patronage issues that affect the prestige of particular political alliances. Foremost among these are the matters of elections and appointments. Thus there is a certain amount of political maneuvering to arrange the distribution of the posts of Assembly Vice Presidents and Committee chairmen. In arranging the states for each session the delegations of the great powers and the major blocs play an important role. These negotiations are considerably facilitated by the planning and coordinating services provided by the Executive Office of the Secretary-General. The groups that are customarily represented on the General Committee, according to a generally understood ratio, are, in addition to the five permanent members of the Security Council, the Commonwealth, Latin America, Europe, Asia, the Soviet group and the Near East.

The most disciplined alliance is of course the Soviet bloc. Next come the Arab and Latin American groups, which have usually worked as units on patronage. The weakest alliances in the Assembly are the Commonwealth, Scandinavian and Benelux groups. Neither the United Kingdom nor France has the circle of close allies that it had in the League. The Asian bloc is just beginning to develop but, with India at its head, it should become increasingly important, especially in connection with eastern problems. The United States frequently receives support from certain states that are obviously dependent upon it, such as the Philippines, Greece and Turkey. At the same time it has not been as successful in influencing the Latin American states as some critics have indicated, notably in connection with the internationalization of Jerusalem and the final vote in the 1948 regular session on the former Italian Colonies.

On the basis of this experience one can see that almost no group, with the exception of the Soviet bloc, maintains unity on all issues. Combinations are reshuffled with far greater freedom than in the usual national legislature. The collaboration of two or more blocs has been most unusual except in matters of elections and appointments. What is disturbing is not the phenomenon of group collaboration, which is to be expected in any political organization, but rather the undue weight in proportion to their real influence which is given to the small states, especially the Latin American group, by the system of equal voting.

Submission of Questions to the Assembly

When Members of the United Nations have submitted political issues to the Assembly they have seldom thought it necessary to cite as justification for such action any particular article of the Charter. Two principal questions concerning which reference was made to specific articles were those regarding the treatment of Indians in South Africa (Articles 10 and 14) and Palestine (Article 10). More frequently Members have not cared to hang their cases on any particular legal pegs. Questions which have been referred to the Assembly with no specific Charter citation have included those concerned with Greece, Korea, the observance in Bulgaria and Hungary of human rights and fundamental freedoms, Indonesia and the Chinese complaint of Soviet intervention. The former Italian Colonies question on the other hand was submitted on the basis of a specific treaty provision, Article 23 and paragraph 3 of Annex XI of the Treaty of Peace with Italy.[4] It should be added, of course, that the absence of any specific reference to the Charter in the original submission of a question has not precluded extensive discussions in the Assembly as to the Articles that are alleged to be relevant.

In some instances questions have been submitted directly to the Assembly without prior reference to the Security Council. In others questions have been transferred as a result of a stalemate in the Council. In a few instances both the Assembly and the Council have dealt concurrently with the same case though generally not with the same aspects of it.

Of the nine specific questions which have been submitted thus far to the Assembly, five plus the pre-hostilities aspects of the Korean situation were given directly to the Assembly without any reference to the Security Council. Two of these items — the treatment of Indians in South Africa and the observance of human rights in Bulgaria, Hungary and Rumania — were submitted to the Assembly by some of the smaller countries because they thought they would win a more sympathetic hearing and more vigorous action in that body than in the Council. On the other hand Iran, Syria, Lebanon and other small states have taken their problems to the Security Council and have received satisfaction. The decision in each case rests partly on the judgment of the plaintiff as to which organ he believes will give him better

---

4 See, respectively, United Nations Docs. A/149, 21 October 1946, A/286, 2 April 1947, A/344, 21 August 1947, A/Bur/85, 17 September 1947, A/820, 18 March 1949 and A/821, 21 March 1949, A/826, 1 April 1949, A/1000, 27 September 1949, and A/645, 16 September 1948.

treatment and also on the advice given him by the great powers, either formally or informally, as to the best course of action.

It is interesting to note that the other four questions which were submitted directly to the Assembly were introduced by great rather than small powers: the former Italian Colonies issue, by the four victorious powers, in accordance with Annex XI of the Italian Peace Treaty which provided for reference to the Assembly in the event that the four could not reach agreement; the independence of Korea, by the United States because it believed that the Soviet Union would block action in the Council; the Chinese complaint of Soviet intervention in China, for the same reason; and the Palestine issue, by the United Kingdom because, as it pointed out, a trusteeship matter belonged rightfully in the Assembly.

Three cases — the Greek, Spanish and Korean hostility questions — were submitted first to the Security Council, but were removed from its agenda after a deadlock made further action impossible. They were then referred to the Assembly. In this connection it is interesting to note that it is not only the non-Soviet nations that have used the Assembly as a court of appeal; it was Poland supported by the Soviet Union which urged that the Spanish question be transferred from the Council to the Assembly. The obvious advantages of transferring a case to the Assembly are the absence of any unanimity rule and the fact that more countries, including important middle as well as small nations, may participate. The disadvantages are that such a move may be considered contrary to the Council's primary responsibility for the maintenance of international peace and security according to Article 24 of the Charter, that it usually antagonizes one or more of the great powers, that it makes possible recommendations by a two-thirds vote of the Assembly which might possibly be contrary to the views of many of the more important powers, and that the Assembly, unlike the Council, does not have the legal authority to use sanctions under Chapter VII of the Charter.

One of the questions that have arisen in connection with the transfer of certain issues from the Security Council to the General Assembly has been the application of Article 12 (1) :

While the Security Council is exercising in respect of any dispute or situation the functions assigned to it in the present Charter, the General Assembly shall not make any recommendations with regard to that dispute or situation unless the Security Council so requests.

In actual practice this provision has not been as serious an obstacle as some observers at San Francisco feared it might. One reason for this is that the members of the Security Council have proceeded on the basis that the removal of an item from the agenda does not require unanimity among the permanent members, as demonstrated in the Greek, Spanish and Korean questions. Another reason is that the Assembly has in several instances made recommendations on subjects which were also being considered by the Security Council.

During the Assembly's third session, for example, a resolution was adopted concerning the Palestine Mediator's report on the current situation while the Security Council was dealing with the problems of the Palestine truce and prospective armistice. When this point was raised by Syria and Egypt during the Assembly debate, the Soviet representative replied that "the Security Council was at present dealing only with the limited questions of the truce and armistice and was not discussing the withdrawal of troops."[5] The Palestine question remained on the Council's agenda. The Assembly also adopted two innocuous resolutions on the Indonesian question while that matter was being dealt with by the Council. The first, during the second part of the Assembly's third session in the spring of 1949, merely deferred further consideration until the fourth session; when that session arrived the following fall, another resolution was

---

[5] Official Records of the Third Session of the General Assembly, Part I, First Committee, Summary Records of Meetings, 21 September-8 December 1948, p. 799.

adopted noting the results of the Hague Conference and welcoming the establishment of the Republic of the United States of Indonesia.

The last instances occurred when the Assembly adopted resolutions on both 7 October 1950, establishing the United Nations Commission for the Unification and Rehabilitation of Korea, and on 14 December 1950, establishing a special three-man cease-fire committee for Korea, while the item, "Complaint of Aggression Upon the Republic of Korea," was still on the agenda of the Security Council. The legal argument again cited to justify this procedure was that the Assembly in these cases was dealing with slightly different aspects of the Korean problem from those being considered by the Council. Actually the Assembly was dealing with the immediate military situation which was also the special concern of the Security Council, as well as certain long-range problems which the Council did not have before it. To avoid all legal doubts, it was decided finally to remove the Korean issue altogether from the Council's agenda before the Assembly adopted the resolution on 1 February 1951, which condemned the intervention in Korea by the People's Republic of China as "aggression." This experience indicates that Article 12 (1) has not thus far been a serious obstacle, both because of the relative ease with which an item may be removed from the Council's agenda and because the Assembly may frequently deal with an item even if it remains on the Council's agenda, on the basis that it is considering a different aspect of the problem.

Advance Documentary Preparation

Another aspect of the submission of questions to the Assembly is the advance preparation of draft resolutions and background material to support these resolutions. Because of the obvious limitations of time and manpower, most delegations, especially the smaller ones, have great difficulty in attempting to master the intricacies of the hundreds of complex issues that confront each session of the Assembly. The quality of advance preparation can therefore be an important factor in determining the quality of the final product.

All too frequently Assembly debates have demonstrated among other things that many of the delegations have not been sufficiently familiar with the plain facts involved. While better documentation will obviously not provide the whole answer to this problem, it would most certainly help. The words of the Interim Committee's Sub-Committee on International Cooperation in the Political Field deserve special emphasis:

Documentation will be useful to the extent that it is authoritative, contemporary and concise.... Careful preparatory work will clarify and have the effect of abbreviating discussions ... in the General Assembly.[6]

Matters previously considered by United Nations organs are supported by the past records and proceedings of those bodies. On the Spanish question and the Greek question, the Security Council directed that "all records and documents of the case be put at the disposal of the General Assembly."[7] When the Interim Committee or special commissions have been authorized to study particular problems, their findings have been an important part of the documentation as in the questions concerning Greece, Korea, the former Italian Colonies and Palestine.

In the League of Nations it was the practice of the Secretariat to distribute, in advance of each Assembly session, documentation on various items on the agenda in the form of a digest of materials submitted by governments and a review of any previous debates and decisions. The only political situation on which the United Nations Secretariat has prepared any extensive material was the Palestine issue, when the following documentary resources were provided:

---

[6] Official Records of the Fifth Session of the General Assembly, Supplement No. 14, Report of the Interim Committee of the General Assembly, p. 11.

[7] See, respectively, Security Council, Official Records, First Year: Second Series, No. 21, p. 498, and Security Council, Official Records, Second Year, No. 89, p. 2401.

(1) A Palestine library including all available official documents and maps as well as unofficial documents and pertinent reference books;

(2) A list of the documents in the Palestine library together with an index by subject matter;

(3) A volume containing a review of various proposals made or considered by governments with a summary of the documents involved; and

(4) A volume containing a factual background survey on Palestine.[8]

Usually however the United Nations Secretariat has not followed the League practice. Yet it is clear that such background material would be a most useful contribution to the Assembly's deliberations.

The difficulties faced by delegations have been further increased in the past by the fact that governments have generally submitted items for the agenda with no supporting material. Two notable exceptions were the relatively comprehensive memoranda provided by the governments of both India and South Africa during the second part of the 1946 session on the treatment of Indians in the Union of South Africa, and the account prepared by the United Kingdom of its mandatory administration of Palestine for the 1947 session.

In order to facilitate adequate advance preparation by governments on the numerous agenda items and to promote informed discussion, the Assembly adopted in 1949 an addition to its Rules of Procedure which became effective 1 January 1950: "All items proposed for inclusion in the agenda shall be accompanied by an explanatory memorandum and, if possible, by basic documents or by a draft resolution."[9] Because of this new rule, there was some improvement during the fifth session in the quantity and quality of supporting documentation.

---

[8] United Nations Doc. A/AC.18/58, 14 May 1948.

[9] Official Records of the Fourth Session of the General Assembly, 20 September-10 December 1949, Resolutions, p. 59.

Advance Diplomatic Negotiations

More important than the documentation, however, is the diplomatic reconnoitering that takes place in preparation for the campaigns in the Assembly. Not only must governments formulate their own national positions on innumerable questions, but they must also begin as early as possible to persuade other United Nations Members to support those positions. When advance consultation is tardy and spotty, the task of gaining broad support during the Assembly session becomes that much more difficult. This was certainly a contributing factor in the skeptical reception which other delegations, friend and foe alike, gave the United States proposal for an interim committee on political questions at the beginning of the second session; the United Kingdom delegation was so disturbed that it felt compelled to indicate publicly that it had not been consulted in advance.[10]

Because of this kind of experience, delegations, especially those of the larger countries, have recently striven to consult earlier, more extensively and more intensively than in the past in order to clear away beforehand as many brambles of avoidable misunderstanding as possible. A significant part of this development has been the increasing tendency on the part of the leading powers such as the United States to include more of the smaller nations in these consultations. In view of the voting strength of the Arab, Asian and Latin American groups and their intimate connection with many of the questions submitted to the Assembly, this development makes eminently good political sense.

This matter of advance diplomatic negotiation also raises the whole question of the sponsorship of resolutions, which is a significant element in the political process of the Assembly. One of the first questions that a member must ask itself is whether or not it wants to propose a resolution directly or work indirectly and discreetly through some other

---

10 See *Official Records of the Second Session of the General Assembly, Plenary Meetings, Verbatim Record, 16 September-29 November 1947*, Vol. I, p. 207.

delegation. The next question is whether to sponsor alone or in collaboration with others. The arguments in favor of individual sponsorship are that it is a simpler method of operating, it reflects more credit upon the single sponsor, it requires less initial compromise, and it avoids offending others when they are not tapped to share in the sponsorship. On the other hand, joint sponsorship creates a team of supporters which not only brings to bear on the formulation of the proposal a number of different points of view, but also encourages far more industrious efforts to achieve victory than if the various states concerned operated separately. These latter considerations were apparent in the decision of the United Kingdom to invite seven other nations to cooperate in sponsoring jointly the resolution concerning the future status of Korea in the fifth session: Australia, Brazil, Cuba, the Netherlands, Norway, Pakistan and the Philippines.[11] When the United States prepared its Uniting for Peace resolution for the fifth session it included as co-sponsors members of the Latin American group (Uruguay), the Asian group (Philippines), and the Near East group (Turkey), as well as its traditional allies, the United Kingdom, France and Canada.[12]

PRELIMINARY CONSIDERATION

Once a political issue is placed on the doorstep of the Assembly, that body must decide whether or not to admit the little stranger and, if it is admitted, what to do with it. Items submitted by members are included in a provisional agenda and communicated by the Secretary-General to the members — 60 days before a regular session, 14 days before a special session requested by the Security Council, 10 days before a special session requested by a majority of the members, and simultaneously with the calling of an emergency special session. Supplementary items submitted at least 30 days before a regular session (four days before a special session) are placed on a supplementary list and communi-

---

11 United Nations Doc. A/C.1/558, 29 September 1950.
12 United Nations Doc. A/C.1/576, 7 October 1950.

cated to the members at least 20 days in advance of a regular session ("as soon as possible" for a special session) . Important "additional items" may also be added just before or during a regular or special session with the express consent of the Assembly. When the Assembly convenes, these lists together with the Secretary-General's proposed allocation of agenda items are presented to the General Committee, which has the responsibility of advising the Assembly whether or not the various items should be included in the agenda.

Efforts to Prevent Consideration

The most frequently cited basis for objecting to Assembly consideration has been the argument that a particular matter lies "essentially within the domestic jurisdiction" of a state and thus beyond United Nations jurisdiction in accordance with Article 2 (7) of the Charter. This tactic has been employed most vigorously in connection with the questions concerning Spain; the treatment of Indians in South Africa; the observance in Bulgaria, Hungary and Rumania of human rights and fundamental freedoms; and Greece. In these discussions the debate has oscillated between liberal and strict interpretations of the language of Article 2 (7). The Assembly has usually settled the matter by proceeding to discuss and adopt resolutions on the substantive issues involved without making any formal declaration regarding the question of competence. In several instances the suggestion has been made by Belgium and others that the issue be submitted to the International Court of Justice for an advisory opinion, but this proposal has never won significant backing. The great majority of the members have been in favor of allowing the Assembly to develop a case-by-case body of precedent with a minimum of formal interpretation of specific Charter provisions. Thus the barrier of "domestic jurisdiction," has not been allowed to be a serious obstacle in the path of the Assembly.

Occasionally some members have invoked Article 12 (1) claiming that the Assembly was not competent to make recommendations concerning a question, although it might discuss it, because the Security Council was seized of the matter, an issue which has already been discussed above. Another periodic complaint has been that to allow the Assembly to assume jurisdiction of a particular matter would be to interfere with the Security Council's "primary responsibility for the maintenance of international peace and security" in accordance with Article 24 (1) of the Charter. This objection was vigorously set forth by the Soviet Union and its friends in opposition to Assembly consideration of the issues regarding Greece, the establishment of the Interim Committee and the Uniting for Peace resolution. Further efforts to bar Assembly action in the political field have been based on restrictive interpretations of Articles 10, 11, 13, 14 and 107 of the Charter. In every one of these instances, however, the Assembly finally decided that it could and should deal with the questions submitted to it.

Rejection or Postponement

This experience reveals no lack of ambition on the part of the Assembly in firmly planting its banner on a great many beachheads. It is almost unheard of for the Assembly to reject a proposed agenda item altogether. It is even rare for the Assembly to decide to postpone the consideration of items as it did in the case of the Arab proposal for the termination of the Palestine Mandate during the first special session and the consideration of the draft declaration of the rights and duties of states during the fifth session.[13] Also during the 1950 session, the General Committee postponed indefinitely a decision on whether or not to recommend that the Assembly should consider the intervention by the People's Republic of China in Tibet.[14]

---

[13] See, respectively, Official Records of the First Special Session of the General Assembly, Vol. I, Plenary Meetings, Verbatim Record, 28 April-15 May 1947, pp. 30-60, and Official Records of the Fifth Session . . . Plenary Meetings, Verbatim Record, pp. 99-103.

[14] Official Records of the Fifth Session . . . General Committee, Summary Records of Meetings, pp. 17-20.

The reasons for the Assembly's reluctance to reject items are obvious enough. First, the language of the Charter is sufficiently elastic so that it has not been difficult to stretch it to accommodate the various issues that have been submitted. Second, the great majority of the members can usually be persuaded to go to the rescue of an alleged "underdog" while the accused has never been able to win sufficient support to prevent Assembly consideration altogether. Third, most "third parties" are reluctant to block issues at the discussion stage although they invariably reserve the right to resist particular courses of action after the discussion has taken place. Fourth, most of the members, especially the smaller states, have favored a tradition of free discussion in order to guarantee for themselves the right of access to the Assembly when they may need assistance.

Role of General Committee

As for the role of the General Committee in recommending what the Assembly should consider, far from being the dictator which some of the smaller countries feared in the beginning, it has been exceedingly liberal. In fact many members have felt that the Committee might well be a sterner watchdog than it has been in the past. Thus the Assembly's Rules were amended in December 1949 to make explicit the Committee's authority to make recommendations concerning the "rejection of the request for inclusion, or the inclusion of the item in the provisional agenda of a future session."[15]

Regarding the suggestion that the International Court of Justice should decide questions of Assembly competence, such a course of action would seem to depend on the individual case. It would obviously be a boon to the evolution of the United Nations if the Members could in time gain sufficient confidence in the Court to accept its opinion on fundamental constitutional questions. This would of course require a greater development not only of the international

---

[15] Rules of Procedure of the General Assembly, 1 January 1950, Rule 40, p. 8.

community but also of the Court itself. Needless to say, this is a development that deserves every encouragement. In the present political environment, however, the prevailing attitude has been that expressed by Committee IV/2 of the San Francisco Conference: that the Charter should be interpreted by each organ concerned and by the Members themselves.[16] It can also be said that, except for basic constitutional questions, other less fundamental issues of this kind should by right be decided by the Assembly as is the practice in any national legislature. Should the majority become too ambitious, the most effective restraint is the majority's own long-range self-interest and the obvious realities of international relations as they have become apparent, for example, in the Spanish and India-South Africa problems.

Besides recommending items for the agenda, the General Committee must also make recommendations to the Assembly concerning the allocation of agenda items to the appropriate committees. Occasionally this matter generates considerable heat since the interested parties are eager to have their items assigned to bodies that are likely to give them sympathetic hearing. On the question concerning the treatment of Indians in South Africa, the latter with the support of the United Kingdom argued spiritedly that since the "legal" question of Assembly competence was of primary importance the matter should be assigned to the Sixth Committee (Legal). On the other hand the Indian delegation supported by the Soviet Union insisted that the principal issue was a "moral" rather than a "legal" one and should be assigned to the First Committee. The United States was willing to split the difference and suggested that the matter be considered by both bodies. Thus it was referred to a Joint Committee of the First and Sixth Committees, the only time when this has been done on a political question.[17] Usually most matters affecting international peace and se-

---

16 UNCIO, Documents, XIII, pp. 703-12.

17 See Official Records of the Second Part of the First Session of the General Assembly, Plenary Meetings, Verbatim Record, 23 October-15 December 1946, pp. 930-31.

curity are assigned either to the First Committee or, beginning with the third session, to an *Ad Hoc* Political Committee.

The General Committee may also recommend that a matter be handled exclusively in plenary meetings of the Assembly without being sent to a main committee. This procedure precludes a certain amount of repetitious debate and relieves the main committees of some of their burden. It has been recommended as

especially appropriate for certain questions the essential aspects of which are already familiar to Members, such as items which have been considered by the General Assembly at previous sessions and which do not require either the presence of representatives of non-member States or the hearing of testimony.[18]

During the first four sessions this method was employed only once, when a political issue was involved, in the first part of the first session in the case of the Spanish question. During the 1950 session, however, three political questions were dealt with in this manner with commendable dispatch: the control of atomic energy, the admission of new members, and the Secretary-General's Twenty-Year Program for Peace.

Once the General Committee has formulated its recommendations they are transmitted to the whole Assembly in plenary session, which normally accepts them. Unfortunately, however, there has been a tendency for the arguments already expressed in the meetings of the General Committee to be let loose again. As a result, the Assembly's Rules were amended during the fourth session to limit the debate to three speakers for and three against the inclusion of an item in the agenda when that item has been recommended for inclusion by the General Committee.[19]

---

18 Rules of Procedure . . . 1950, Annex II, p. 35.
19 Official Records of the Fourth Session . . . Resolutions, p. 60.

SUBSTANTIVE CONSIDERATION

General Debate

The grand strategy regarding the substance of the various political issues submitted to the Assembly is usually revealed during the general debate which takes place in the plenary meetings at the beginning of the session. No one has better described this procedure than the Soviet Union's Mr. Vyshinsky in his initial address during the 1950 session:

The General Assembly has begun its work, as always, by holding a general debate, in which it is customary to draw up the balance of the activities of the United Nations during the preceding year and to outline new problems and the methods of solving them. The general debate gives every delegation an opportunity to express its views on the questions which interest the Assembly and to state its position with regard to the proposals and plans submitted to the Assembly.[20]

During this exchange all eyes are upon the chief figures in the drama, especially the representatives of the great powers, as they deliver their keynote speeches.

At the beginning of the fifth session, for example, there can be no doubt that the most carefully audited pronouncements were those delivered to a capacity audience by Messrs. Acheson and Vyshinsky as the second and third speakers, respectively, in the general debate which began the afternoon of 20 September 1950. Mr. Acheson first analyzed certain basic contemporary world problems, with particular emphasis on issues concerning the Soviet Union, and then went on to outline briefly the United States positions on the proposed Uniting for Peace resolution, Korea, Formosa, control of atomic energy and certain related economic and social measures. Mr. Vyshinsky, after saying that the Soviet Union believed in peace and the United Nations more than any other nation, especially the United States, went on to present his country's views on China, Korea, arms regulation and

---

[20] Official Records of the Fifth Session . . . Plenary Meetings, Verbatim Record, p. 27.

war propaganda. Then he read the entire text of a Soviet Union resolution entitled "Declaration on the Removal of the Threat of a New War and the Strengthening of Peace and Security Among the Nations."[21] This presentation by the Soviet Union of an omnibus peace resolution during the general debate has become a kind of Assembly tradition which started in the second part of the 1946 session when the Soviet Union waited until the opening of the session to present its surprise disarmament resolution. While these annual peace plans gave rise to considerable excitement and optimism in earlier sessions, they have been greeted more recently with a certain degree of cynicism.

Functions of the President

It is important also to recognize the strategic role which is played by the President of the Assembly not only in helping to give direction to the general debate, but to the entire session. His formal functions have been substantial from the very beginning and they were reinforced as a result of the revision of the Assembly's Rules in December 1949. He now has considerable authority to regulate the operations of the Assembly, including the coordination of the activities of the committees of the Assembly. According to the Rules of Procedure the General Committee has the responsibility of assisting the President "in determining the priority of . . . items and in the co-ordination of the proceedings of all committees. . . ."[22] In actual practice the General Committee is so hampered by current international tensions that it has proved relatively ineffective in reaching practical decisions on the scheduling and coordination of the committees' work. Thus the Executive Assistant to the Secretary-General, Andrew Cordier, who is especially concerned with this aspect of Assembly organization, has developed the informal device of a weekly luncheon meeting attended by the President of the Assembly, the committee chairmen, and one or two

---

21 United Nations Doc. A/1376, 20 September 1950.
22 Rules of Procedure . . . 1950, Rule 41, p. 8.

people from Mr. Cordier's office. Fortunately this body, in which the Assembly Vice Presidents (including the great power delegates) are not represented, has managed to fill the gap left by the General Committee and, in view of present international difficulties, is probably the best means of performing these functions.

Even more important than the President's formal duties, however, are the functions which he frequently performs which are not mentioned in the Rules. Herbert Evatt, for example, describes in his book, *The Task of Nations,* the appeal which he made on behalf of the Assembly during the first part of the third session, in cooperation with the Secretary-General, to the United States, the United Kingdom, the Soviet Union and France to make special efforts to settle the Berlin crisis amicably.[23] During the disarmament debate in the second part of the first session, Paul-Henri Spaak exerted his influence with telling effect behind the scenes in assisting the various interested parties to formulate a satisfactory compromise. Frequently the Presidents have been asked to engage in special pacific settlement efforts. For example, Mr. Evatt was authorized to conduct during both parts of the third session intensive negotiations with the states directly involved in the Greek question and Mr. Entezam was asked during the fifth session to participate in a three-man committee to attempt to negotiate a cease-fire in Korea. In his key position as the central and most important officer of the Assembly the President is inevitably drawn into the vortex of every major issue submitted to the Assembly. Fortunately the men who have been elected to the position thus far have for the most part been able men who have provided remarkably effective leadership in the face of the most diverse and atomistic forces imaginable.

Committee Debate

As the general debate comes to a close the main committees begin to give detailed consideration to the individual

---

23 (New York, Duell, Sloan and Pearce, 1949), pp. 83-84.

agenda items, except for those few matters which are handled entirely in plenary meetings as noted above. Compared to the committees of the usual national legislature, Assembly committees seem exceptionally cumbersome, particularly because the full membership of the United Nations is represented in each of them. Since there is no party machinery to bind the delegations together in convenient bundles, except for certain unpredictable and relatively undisciplined blocs, there are sixty separate "parties" whose interests must be reconciled. Fortunately not all of these members try to speak on every issue, but the temptations of national and personal pride are always present and not easy to resist. The debate seems slow and disjointed since speeches are usually prepared far enough in advance to allow time for necessary governmental clearance. Thus there can be little free give-and-take except towards the end of the discussion on a particular issue when the basic governmental positions are established and only minor changes are involved.

In spite of these difficulties, however, the Assembly has developed various rules and procedures designed to make the apparatus run as smoothly as possible within the framework established by the Charter. Inevitably any body in which the centrifugal pressures are as insistent as they are in an Assembly committee must rely to a large extent on the unifying influence of a strong leader. Thus the chairman of a committee is authorized according to the Assembly's Rules to

direct ... discussions, ensure observance of ... rules, accord the right to speak, put questions and announce decisions, ... rule on points of order and ... have complete control of the proceedings of the committee and over the maintenance of order at its meetings. The Chairman may ... propose to the committee the limitation of the time to be allowed to speakers, the limitation of the number of times each representative may speak on any question, the closure of the list of speakers or the closure of the debate. He may also propose the suspension or the adjournment of the meeting or the adjournment of the debate on the item under discussion.[24]

---

24 Rules of Procedure ... 1950, Rule 106, p. 19.

While the chairman's rulings, like those of the President of the Assembly, may be challenged by any delegation and over-ruled by a simple majority vote, he has sufficient authority so that with courage, tact, and a sixth sense of what the group will is at any moment, he is in a position to expedite the deliberations considerably.

The Assembly's Rules are silent, however, with respect to some of the most significant functions which tend to gravitate into the hands of the chairman. Perhaps the most important, and certainly the most delicate, task of the chairman is that of conciliation in some form or other. The chairman of the First Committee, for example, served on conciliation committees to meet with representatives of the four states directly interested in the Greek case during the first part of the third session and also the fourth session.[25] In the First Committee, during the first part of the third session, in connection with the repatriation of Greek children, the chairman not only assumed the initiative in suggesting a compromise plan involving the use of the Red Cross as a neutral agent, but was actually authorized by the Committee, including the Yugoslav and Greek delegations, to draft a proposal which was finally adopted.[26] Another closely related task frequently assigned to the chairman is that of suggesting specific states and individuals to comprise various Assembly commissions. It is difficult to emphasize sufficiently the central importance of this function since the character of the membership of these bodies exerts such a direct influence upon their effectiveness.

It is obvious therefore that the ability of the chairman, and to a lesser extent of the vice chairman and rapporteur, is a major factor in the operations of a committee. Unfortunately certain forces operate to make it difficult for these

---

[25] Official Records of the Third Session ... Part I, First Committee, Summary Records ... p. 541, and Official Records of the Fourth Session ... First Committee, Summary Records of Meetings, 20 September - 6 December 1949, p. 9.

[26] Official Records of the Third Session ... Part I, First Committee, Summary Records ... p. 495.

posts always to be placed in the most capable hands. To begin with, a tradition, begun in the League of Nations, reserves the chairmanships of the main committees for the smaller countries. At the same time these states can ill afford to allow the time of their most able representatives to be absorbed entirely by the task of chairmanship rather than being devoted to the promotion of particular national interests. The diplomatic tensions involved in the task, especially in a body such as the First Committee, also discourage some individuals from accepting the post. Finally certain bloc pressures have compelled the Assembly to adopt as part of its rules governing the selection of committee chairmen the criterion of "equitable geographic distribution" as well as "experience and personal competence." In the past some exceptionally capable men have been made chairmen of the various bodies concerned with political issues; other less able men in these posts have actually handicapped the Assembly's work.

Besides the question of committee leadership there are the traffic rules which have been established to regulate the flow of negotiation. The priority of agenda items to be discussed is left for the most part to the discretion of each Committee. Unfortunately a considerable amount of time has frequently been devoted to this matter as various interest groups jockey for position. The priority of speakers is determined by the order in which they request permission from the chairman. Debate on a particular item is usually initiated by the sponsor and other members who are directly concerned. When South Africa insisted, during the second part of the third session, that it had been the first to indicate a desire to speak, although the sponsor was India, the First Committee decided to allow India to begin the discussion.[27] All procedural questions concerning such matters as closing the list of speakers, closure or adjournment of debate, and miscellaneous points

---

[27] Official Records of the Third Session of the General Assembly, Part II, First Committee, Summary Records of Meetings, 6 April-10 May 1949, pp. 246-53.

of order are decided by a simple majority of those present and voting; abstentions are not considered voting. Draft resolutions and amendments are normally required to be submitted in writing to the Secretariat in time for copies to be circulated to all delegations not later than the day before the meeting when they are to be discussed, although the chairman is authorized to make exceptions.

Many delegates have complained about the number of times that individual delegates are allowed to speak and the excessive length of some of the speeches. While they recognize and are resigned to many of the factors that make it impossible at present for the international assembly to be as disciplined as some national legislatures, they believe that a minimum degree of improvement is possible and desirable. To support their case they cite as one example the debate on the Greek question during the first part of the third session which consisted of a total of 764 speeches of which thirteen were more than half an hour in length. Although the original Rules of the Assembly provided that a committee might "limit the time to be allowed to each speaker," no one, including the chairman, was ever eager to impose such a limitation upon his fellow-delegates. To tighten the procedure a bit the Assembly authorized in December 1949 an additional limitation upon "the number of times each representative may speak on any question" and added a provision to encourage the chairman to be more exacting: "When the debate is limited and a representative has spoken his allotted time, the Chairman shall call him to order without delay."[28] Some delegates still believe, however, that the emphasis of the Rules should be changed so that a blanket limitation would be applied to all speeches, as is the practice in the International Labour Organisation, thus placing the onus upon those who might wish to extend the debate. Certainly the present strain upon the Assembly's time and manpower would seem to justify giving careful consideration to this proposal.

---

[28] Rules of Procedure . . . 1950, Rule 113, p. 20.

Non-Member Participation

Another important aspect of the political process of the Assembly is the extent to which it reaches beyond the circle of its own members to deal with (1) non-member states, (2) *de facto* authorities, (3) non-governmental organizations, and (4) inter-governmental organizations. In the Assembly's relations with these groups the first questions that arise in each case are: what groups should be permitted access to the Assembly and under what conditions? Neither the Rules of Procedure nor the Charter discusses the conditions which should govern outside participation in Assembly discussions except under Article 35 (2):

A state which is not a Member of the United Nations may bring to the attention of the Security Council or of the General Assembly any dispute to which it is a party if it accepts in advance, for the purposes of the dispute, the obligations of pacific settlement provided in the present Charter.

Although this passage allows a non-member to approach the Assembly under certain circumstances, it does not guarantee that the Assembly will entertain the request nor does it apply to an authority which is not a "state." Furthermore it does not deal with the rights of non-member parties to a dispute when that dispute is referred to the Assembly by someone else, nor does it apply to a question which is not a "dispute."

When the Greek question was discussed in the First Committee during the second session, the Soviet bloc argued that the Assembly should recognize an obligation similar to that of the Security Council in accordance with Article 32 of the Charter:

Any Member of the United Nations which is not a member of the Security Council or any state which is not a Member of the United Nations, if it is a party to a dispute under consideration by the Security Council, shall be invited to participate, without vote, in the discussion relating to the dispute. The Security Council shall lay down such conditions as it deems just for the participation of a state which is not a Member of the United Nations.

At the same time the Soviet Union declared that the conditions attached to invitations by the Security Council should not be applied "automatically" to the Assembly.[29] The Committee finally decided to ask Albania and Bulgaria if their governments were prepared "to agree to apply the principles and rules of the Charter in the settlement of the Greek question."[30] Both states replied that they would insist on an absolute right to be heard, free of all conditions. Finally the Committee adopted a Belgian proposal to invite the two countries to participate to the extent of making "statements ... on the Greek question" and to replying "to any questions which may be put to them."[31]

Usually invitations have been sent in response to a specific request to be heard although the Assembly has also virtually summoned states by assuming the initiative in inviting them to appear to answer questions. Thus the *Ad Hoc* Political Committee "invited" representatives of Bulgaria and Hungary "to participate without vote in the discussion" of the observance of human rights in those countries although they themselves had indicated no desire to participate.[32] This decision was not accepted without a certain amount of resistance on the part of some delegations who believed that under the circumstances invitations should be issued only upon request. Nor was the strategy successful since the recipients of the invitation refused to comply.

In the case of *de facto* authorities and non-governmental organizations an important consideration is to ascertain their representative character. Various methods have been proposed from time to time to assist the Assembly in deciding what organizations should be heard. One device has been to depend on the findings of a special field commission. Thus the First Committee during the first part of the third session

---

29 Official Records of the Second Session ... First Committee, Summary Record of Meetings, 16 September-19 November 1947, p. 11.

30 *Ibid.*, p. 12.

31 *Ibid.*, p. 31.

32 Official Records of the Third Session ... Part II, *Ad Hoc* Political Committee, Summary Records of Meetings, 6 April-10 May 1949, p. 65.

based its decision to invite the government of the Republic of Korea to participate on the report of the United Nations Temporary Commission on Korea.[33]

Another source of information has been the experience of states especially acquainted with particular areas: the United Kingdom on Palestine; Egypt, Italy, the United Kingdom and others on the former Italian Colonies; and the United States on Korea. A third method has been to establish special sub-committees to make recommendations on the hearing of non-governmental bodies. Thus the First Committee appointed a sub-committee which considered thirteen requests to testify on the Palestine question and unanimously decided to recommend the rejection of all of them.[34] Another similar sub-committee in connection with the former Italian Colonies was far more lenient; while recognizing that "not . . . all the . . . parties and organizations represented a substantial section of opinion in the territories concerned, and . . . at the same time that the data available were incomplete and contradictory and that therefore the claims of these bodies could not be clearly substantiated,"[35] the committee nevertheless decided to give the organizations the benefit of the doubt and recommend that they be heard. Even when groups have not been allowed to make oral statements, however, their written communications to the Assembly have invariably been brought to the attention of the delegations.

Besides the question of who should participate, there is the question of how the participation should be organized. In this connection two broad principles are generally observed. First, no non-member may cast a vote in the Assembly. Second, participation should be restricted in time and place to those phases of an Assembly discussion in which the outsider

---

[33] Official Records of the Third Session . . . Part I, First Committee, Summary Records . . . p. 955.

[34] Official Records of the First Special Session . . . Vol. III, Main Committees, Verbatim Records of Meetings, 28 April-13 May 1947, p. 165.

[35] Official Records of the Third Session . . . Part II, First Committee, Annexes to the Summary Records of Meetings 1949, p. 18.

is directly concerned. While non-members have regularly been excluded from participating in plenary meetings of the Assembly, they have been allowed to participate in the discussions of the main committees and their sub-committees under the conditions set forth above. The degree of participation varies according to the circumstances and is usually indicated in general terms in the invitation to the outside participant. The First Committee's invitation to Italy to join the discussion on the former Italian Colonies indicated that the Italian delegate would be allowed to

sit, without vote, during the Committee's consideration of the question . . . , such representative to be present for the purpose of answering questions, providing such assistance as the Committee may require and making an initial statement, as well as such further statements as the Committee may consider appropriate.[36]

In general the Assembly has granted some combination of three possible forms of participation: (1) the making of statements, (2) answering questions, and (3) replying to accusations. The participant has of course the right to refuse to answer any question put to him.

The Assembly's willingness to open its doors to all of these non-members is a measure of its flexibility and its extensive influence beyond the confines of its own membership. In the case of non-member states, this procedure makes it possible for the Assembly to develop limited relations with nations such as Italy which have not yet been admitted to full membership in the United Nations. In the case of non-governmental organizations, the Assembly is able to establish closer relations with various groups of people than if it were to work exclusively through governments.

At the same time there are obvious difficulties. The Assembly frequently expects that non-members should be willing to accept the obligations of the Charter when they participate. Unfortunately many of them do not and will not. Furthermore the present members are in a position to

---

[36] *Ibid.*, p. 2.

exclude their enemies from participation. Thus the United States and others have at various times strongly resisted allowing the People's Republics of China and North Korea to join Assembly discussions. The First Committee did however decide during the fifth session to allow a representative of the People's Republic of China to "present his views and provide such information as the Committee may request during the discussion of the item 'Complaint by the USSR Regarding Aggression Against China by the United States of America' " without mentioning the principles of the Charter.[37]

One significant aspect of such cases is that regimes like the People's Republics of China and Korea have indicated a lively interest in gaining access to the Assembly debates because they believe that those debates are an important political force. To take advantage of this motivation and to invite these authorities to participate is one means of building a bridge between them and the United Nations. To hear them is of course not to approve their views. If they choose to distort the facts, there are ways of counteracting their statements, especially by means of the reports of multilateral United Nations field commissions such as those that have operated in Korea and Greece. In the case of many nongovernmental groups, however, it is especially difficult to ascertain their representative character. In these instances it would seem advisable to establish sub-committees to study the situation carefully and to screen the groups accordingly. The same bodies might also hear the evidence and present an appraisal to the main committee rather than using the time of the whole membership, which is usually not sufficiently informed to weigh the testimony properly. Many delegations felt that the numerous and lengthy statements which were made before the entire First Committee in connection with the former Italian Colonies did not justify the considerable amount of time which they consumed.

---

[37] Official Records of the Fifth Session...First Committee, Summary Records of Meetings, p. 384.

Use of Sub-Committees

This mention of one use of sub-committees raises the whole problem of how best to relieve the main committees of part of their burden through the judicious use of sub-bodies. These smaller groups play a strategic role in the work of the Assembly and are more nearly comparable to the usual standing committees of national legislatures than are the Assembly's main committees. Since there are no permanent sub-bodies under the main committees, their establishment on an *ad hoc* basis with respect to various agenda items usually involves considerable discussion concerning both their authority and organization.

In general there are three broad functions that have been assigned to sub-committees. One important task has been that of harmonizing various points of view in order to arrive at a compromise solution. This may take the form of working directly with the parties to a dispute, as in the case of the sub-committees formed during the third and fourth sessions to deal with the Greek question. Another form of this same function has been to reconcile various draft resolutions introduced before the main committee. Thus several sub-committees were organized during various sessions to struggle with the many proposals concerning the former Italian Colonies.

In formulating the mandates of these sub-bodies the obvious difficulty that arises is the question of how stringently to limit their discretion. Delegations fearing that their views may not be adequately represented or wanting to restrict the scope of the negotiations usually insist on explicit and rigid instructions. During the discussion on recognition in the *Ad Hoc* Political Committee during the fifth session, the United Kingdom representative insisted that a sub-committee should not be formed until "precise and clear" instructions had been formulated to govern its deliberations.[38] On the other hand the United Kingdom was quite content

---

[38] Official Records of the Fifth Session ... *Ad Hoc* Political Committee, Summary Records of Meetings, 30 September-14 December 1950, p. 124.

to approve a conveniently elastic mandate for Sub-Committee 15 established by the First Committee during the second part of the third session to consider in connection with the former Italian Colonies the "various proposals which have been submitted or may be submitted" and to draft a compromise resolution.[39] Through this wide door the United Kingdom was able to introduce the so-called Bevin-Sforza plan which had never been discussed before the First Committee.

A second function often delegated to sub-committees is that of nominating states and individuals for special assignments under the authority of the Assembly. For example, the First Committee appointed sub-committees, composed of representatives of the states which are permanent members of the Security Council, to select both the Palestine Mediator during the second special session and the Palestine Conciliation Commission during the third session. In the fourth session it was the First Committee's Sub-Committee 17 which suggested the composition of the Libya Advisory Council as part of the compromise proposal which it drafted.[40] Frequently, however, many states want to wait until the mandate of a field commission is thoroughly agreed upon and approved before negotiating concerning the membership of that commission.

The third function assigned to sub-committees is that of screening the requests of non-member groups wishing to testify before a main committee such as the sub-bodies established in connection with Palestine and the former Italian Colonies which were discussed above.

As for the organization of sub-committees, one of the most important questions always to be faced is: what interests are to be represented? It is obvious that if the sub-committee is to be politically realistic, its membership must reflect the general pattern of interests of the main committee. Yet that pattern is far from stable except for one or two rather rigid

---

[39] Official Records of the Third Session . . . Part II, First Committee, Summary Records . . . p. 271 and United Nations Doc. A/C.1/459, 9 May 1949.
[40] United Nations Doc. A/C.1/522, 1 November 1949.

blocs. The usual procedure is first of all to include the great powers, a fact which significantly reinforces their influence in the Assembly since much of the most important negotiation and drafting takes place in sub-committees. This procedure recognizes the obvious influence of the great powers, especially on security matters, and helps to compensate for the unrealistic equality of representation in the Assembly as a whole. During the second session discussions on Palestine, for example, it was the United States, the United Kingdom and the Soviet Union operating in various sub-bodies that largely determined the form of the compromises which were reported to the First Committee.[41]

Besides the great powers, those countries that have submitted specific proposals or are otherwise directly concerned are usually included. If the matter is of general interest an effort is also made to include the various area interests more or less according to their relative strength in the Assembly. Thus the *Ad Hoc* Political Committee's sub-committee on criteria of recognition during the fifth session consisted of the permanent members of the Security Council plus five members from Latin America (Argentina, Cuba, Dominican Republic, Uruguay and Venezuela), one from the Pacific area (Australia), one from Europe (Belgium), one from the Middle East (Egypt), one from Asia (India), and one from the Soviet bloc (Poland).[42]

Another consideration that affects the organization of sub-committees is the question of timing. In some instances, such as the fifth session discussion on criteria of recognition, the United States urged early consideration of the issue by a sub-committee "before it was discussed extensively" by the *Ad Hoc* Political Committee so that the latter might subsequently have the advantage of "well-considered information and a maximum reconciliation of views."[43] It was obvious that a sub-committee would be more conducive than

---

[41] United Nations Doc. A/C.14/34, 19 November 1947.
[42] Official Records of the Fifth Session ... *Ad Hoc* Political Committee, Summary Records ... p. 160.
[43] *Ibid.*, p. 120.

the main committee to relatively free discussion and compromise. It would also allow the item to be shunted to a side-track so that other matters might be dealt with by the main body. On the other hand, during the same debate the United Kingdom expressed the need for full general debate on the subject by the entire committee so that the subcommittee might be given clear and explicit instructions.[44]

The suggestion for the establishment of a sub-committee has also been looked upon as a means of obstructing, or at least delaying, the formulation of a policy. During the fifth session debate on Korea in the First Committee, when India proposed a sub-committee to work out a compromise, especially between the United States and the Soviet Union, the United States strongly opposed the move as a needless delay that could not produce a compromise and would merely sacrifice more lives in the Korean hostilities.[45]

While it is difficult to measure the general effectiveness of sub-committees, a survey of the results of all sub-committee proposals on political issues through the fifth session indicates that the great majority of them have been adopted in some form or other. On the whole they have produced useful and acceptable compromises. There is little doubt that the judicious use of sub-committees, properly directed and organized, is one of the best ways to provide extra eyes, arms and legs for the main committees. The smaller membership and off-the-record atmosphere of these sub-bodies make them particularly useful devices for conciliation and other forms of specialized negotiation. It is obvious of course that "going into sub-committee" sometimes invites a far more intensive sifting of the issues and detailed drafting than is usually attempted in the full committee. Naturally the better the advance negotiation and drafting is, the less necessary should be the use of sub-bodies. Since the utilization of sub-committees is a definite strain upon the manpower resources of delegations, particularly the smaller ones, they should not be

---

44 *Ibid.,* p. 124.
45 *Ibid.,* First Committee, Summary Records . . . p. 55.

organized except when there is general agreement that they will serve some practical purpose. It is also important that their membership be so selected that they reflect the major interest blocs of the Assembly in order that their recommendations will receive sympathetic consideration by the parent body.

Voting Procedures

When the debate is concluded and the compromises have been made, the time arrives for voting, first in committee and then in plenary meetings.[46] Since voting in the Assembly is not impeded by a "veto" and since the decisions voted on are not legally binding, with the exception of budget questions and some extraordinary arrangement such as the Italian Colonies settlement, the voting rules have not given rise to the intense disputes that have taken place in connection with Security Council voting. In committee all decisions are made by a simple majority, except for a special two-thirds requirement when voting to reconsider a decision; whereas, in plenary meetings all "important questions" require a two-thirds majority.

The principal reason for the more flexible committee procedure is that it makes it relatively easy to reach a decision, thus expediting negotiations. The expectation is that once a conclusion has been reached in committee many states which have opposed the majority view up to the bitter end will probably reconsider and decide to jump on the bandwagon. While this has been the usual pattern on political questions, there have been notable occasions when a weak majority decision of the committee did not win two-thirds of the votes in the plenary meeting, such as the First Committee's abortive proposals on the former Italian Colonies and on the Spanish question during the second part of the third session. During the 1950 session also, the First Committee's decision

---

46 For discussion of several major issues, see Allan Hovey, Jr., "Voting Procedure in the General Assembly," *International Organization*, Vol. IV, No. 3 (August, 1950), pp. 412-27.

on Jerusalem failed to win approval in plenary session. The obvious disadvantage of the simple majority voting procedure in committee is that it does not compel the members to formulate a compromise which has the support of two-thirds of the votes before going to the plenary meeting. If the committee recommendation is finally defeated in plenary it is too late to try for a new compromise.

In committee, as well as in plenary,. various views have been expressed as to the interpretation of the last three words of the first sentence in Article 18 (1) of the Charter: "Decisions . . . shall be made by a . . . majority of the members present and voting." Paul-Henri Spaak of Belgium was the first President of the Assembly to have to decide whether abstentions were to be considered votes or not. This was an important decision since, if they were to count as votes, a larger affirmative majority would be required to approve a proposal than if they were not. M. Spaak insisted that they should be considered votes; if not, a ridiculously small number of votes could win the decision. Mr. Wellington Koo and others argued that such an interpretation was not intended by the framers of the Charter and would make the voting procedure unnecessarily rigid. It was this latter view that was finally adopted by the Assembly, a decision which M. Spaak found rather painful to swallow.[47] In defense of the Assembly's position it should be said that members always have the right to vote against a measure if they so desire. If they abstain they do so with the knowledge that they run the risk of allowing the proposal to be carried by a very small majority.

The procedures governing voting in committee are essentially the same as those in plenary. Any delegate may request a roll-call, which is frequently done to remind members that the eyes of God and their fellow-men are upon them, to make one's own record clear at home, and also as a filibuster tactic to delay the proceedings. When two or more amendments

---

[47] Paul-Henri Spaak, "The Role of the General Assembly," *International Conciliation*, No. 445 (November, 1948), pp. 603-04.

are being considered, the committee votes first "on the amendment furthest removed in substance from the original proposal . . . "[48] which requires a chairman with a fine eye for judging distances and frequently gives rise to some lively discussions. Proposals may also be voted on by parts. Under earlier Rules there were doubts as to whether it was necessary to vote on a measure as a whole after all of its parts had been defeated individually, a fate which seemed to befall resolutions proposed by the Soviet Union more than any other member. The revised Rules of 1 January 1950 now make it clear that "if all operative parts . . . have been rejected, the proposal or amendment shall be considered to have been rejected as a whole."[49] The Rule governing the order of voting on two or more individual resolutions is relatively simple; they are normally to be dealt with in the order in which they have been submitted.

When, in the past, proposals approved by a main committee have been submitted to the Assembly in plenary session, considerable time has frequently been devoted to a recital of all the arguments previously voiced in the committee and, before that, in the preliminary plenary discussion and the General Committee. This became the customary pattern in connection with such controversial political issues as those concerning Greece, Palestine, Spain and Korea. In an effort to stem this excessive flood of oratory, there was general agreement during the fourth session that greater advantage should be taken of the Rule that the report of a main committee shall take place only if at least one-third of the members present and voting decide that such a discussion is "necessary."[50] During the fifth session, however, when one-third of the members did not approve a discussion, the Soviet Union and other delegations that had strongly opposed the new emphasis used their right to "explain their votes" as a means of discussing the substance of the committee reports. Nevertheless the new effort noticeably reduced

---

[48] Rules of Procedure . . . 1950, Rule 129, p. 23.
[49] *Ibid.*, Rule 128, p. 23.
[50] *Ibid.*, Rule 67, p. 12.

the volume of debate in plenary meetings during the fifth session.

It is in plenary session, of course, that the strongest pressure is exerted by the supporters of a proposal to produce as large a majority as possible. Frequent statements are made that a strong majority will promote more effective results; lobbying is intense; and frequent roll-calls are requested. In connection with the requirement of a two-thirds majority on "important questions," the members have occasionally debated whether a particular issue was an "important question." Article 18 of the Charter lists as important matters which require a two-thirds majority:

recommendations with respect to the maintenance of international peace and security, the election of the non-permanent members of the Security Council, the election of the members of the Economic and Social Council, the election of members of the Trusteeship Council . . . , the admission of new Members to the United Nations, the suspension of the rights and privileges of membership, the expulsion of Members, questions relating to the operation of the trusteeship system, and budgetary questions.

During the debate on the treatment of Indians in South Africa in the second part of the first session, the Indian delegation, which was in favor of the resolution before the Assembly, argued that it was not a question which should require a two-thirds vote. The South African delegation, which was opposed to the resolution, insisted that it was a recommendation with respect to the maintenance of international peace and security and in accordance with Article 18 of the Charter should require a two-thirds majority. The Assembly finally decided in favor of the latter point of view.[51] In arriving at this decision the Assembly purposely avoided making any decision on general principles but restricted itself solely to the issue of what majority should be required on the specific question then before the Assembly. In general one might say that a question does not require a

---

[51] Official Records of the Second Part of the First Session . . . Plenary Meetings, Verbatim Record . . . p. 1060.

two-thirds majority unless it can reasonably be said to come within one of the categories listed in Article 18 or unless new categories are created, which thus far has never been done. While new categories may be added by a simple majority vote, in accordance with Article 18 (3) of the Charter, those already explicitly provided for in Article 18 (2) may not be altered except by amending the Charter. For the most part there has been relatively little controversy on this issue in connection with political questions since the members have usually agreed, implicitly if not explicitly, that such questions naturally fall within the category of "recommendations with respect to the maintenance of international peace and security."

A closely related issue is: should amendments to and decisions on separate parts of important questions voted on in plenary session also require a two-thirds majority? The practice through the fifth session was to allow such proposals to be approved by a simple majority in order to permit more flexible negotiation and compromise than would otherwise have been possible. The disadvantage of this procedure was of course that modifications might be calculated to alter the original proposal to such an extent that it would lose rather than gain support. After a futile attempt in the fourth session to alter this procedure, the Assembly finally succeeded during the fifth session in amending the Rules to read:

Decisions of the General Assembly on amendments to proposals relating to important questions, and on parts of such proposals put to the vote separately, shall be taken by a two-thirds majority of the Members present and voting.[52]

Weighted Voting

Besides these questions concerning the procedure of Assembly voting, there is also the perennial debate as to the desirability of some form of weighted voting. The experi-

---

[52] Official Records of the Fifth Session...Plenary Meetings, Verbatim Record, p. 290.

ence of the Assembly since the San Francisco Conference has not reduced the belief in some quarters that the plenary body would be a more realistic and a more useful organization if its voting procedure reflected more accurately the relative importance of countries in terms of such criteria as population and economic development. In 1948 Paul-Henri Spaak said,

I do not think that Belgium plays the same role in international politics as the United States. I do not think that an organization such as that of the United Nations will really be able to function well if it is based upon a system that is clearly unreal. For myself, I can quite well conceive of establishing some sort of qualified vote and quantitative vote, and of having each nation in the General Assembly and later in the Security Council vote in a manner that might be described as "weighted."[53]

John Foster Dulles wrote in his recent book, *War or Peace,*

... the weight of its [Assembly] recommendations would be far greater if the votes reflected not merely numbers but also ability to contribute to the maintenance of international peace and security. ...

I would not abolish, in the United Nations, an Assembly vote which, like that of our Senate, reflects the sovereign equality of all nations. ... But there might be introduced, in addition, a system of "weighted" voting. ... Then it should be provided that decisions on important matters would require a simple majority, rather than two-thirds, under each of the two voting procedures.[54]

General Carlos Romulo of the Philippines and others have voiced similar views.[55]

Unfortunately certain obvious technical and, what are far more important, political obstacles stand in the way. Many small countries, in spite of the sentiments of Messrs. Spaak,

---

[53] *Op. cit.,* p. 601.
[54] (New York, Macmillan, 1950) , pp. 191-92.
[55] Official Records of the Second Part of the First Session ... First Committee, Summary Record of Meetings, 2 November-13 December 1946, pp. 102-03.

Romulo, Berendsen and a few others, still resist any diminution in the present weight of their votes. Large industrial countries such as the United States and the United Kingdom look askance at any change that might favor the huge populations of China and India. The anti-communist countries also disapprove of any move that might give the Soviet bloc more strength than it has at present. The Soviet minority on the other hand wants no reform that will make the majority even stronger than it is at present. The view has been expressed by some USSR authorities as late as 1949 that any move in the direction of weighted voting smacks of the "world parliament" school of thought which would weaken the authority of individual states and would also detract from the present role of the Security Council in which the Soviet Union together with the other permanent members holds a very advantageous position.[56] Yet, in an interview reported on 17 February 1951, Premier Stalin was quoted as complaining that "the small Dominican Republic . . . has the same weight in the United Nations as India . . . ."[57] Many states are hesitant to propose any reform which would require amendment of the Charter for fear of opening a Pandora's box that might get out of control. At present, therefore, no serious official consideration is being given to the possibility of introducing a formal system of weighted voting in the Assembly. This is such a key problem, however, that it would seem to justify new efforts in both governmental and non-governmental circles to explore means of providing a more satisfactory reflection of undeniable differences in strength and influence among the Members.

At the same time it is important to recognize the fact, which many observers overlook, that an unofficial informal system of weighted voting is already in operation. Behind the mythical mask of equality it is all too obvious that the more important states wield an influence in actual fact that

---

[56] S. B. Krylov, *Materialy k Istorii Organizatsii Ob'edinennykh Natsii* (Moscow, Izdatel'stvo Akademii Nauk SSR, 1949) (unpublished translation), pp. 160-63.

[57] *The New York Times,* 17 February 1951, p. 3.

is roughly commensurate with their relative weight in world politics. There are, for example, certain institutional devices which give special consideration to the views of the more important powers. Representatives of the great powers are invariably appointed, whenever they so desire, to the various Assembly sub-committees and commissions, as well as to special posts such as the Assembly vice-presidencies which give them seats on the General Committee. The more influential middle powers such as Canada, Australia, India, Brazil, Argentina, the Netherlands, etc., also tend to be favored although not to the same degree. A second important way in which votes are weighted informally is by "attraction." As pointed out earlier, the more influential powers inevitably tend to draw into their orbits smaller countries that are in varying degrees dependent upon them.

The fact that the votes of certain influential delegations "weigh more" than others in terms of their political influence has a very direct bearing upon the relative effectiveness of various Assembly resolutions. The impact of a decision made by any governmental institution depends not only on its formal character as a "law" or "recommendation," but also on such additional factors as the quality, quantity and intensity of the community support which stands behind it. Although the federal prohibition acts which the United States attempted to enforce at one time were legally "binding," that was not enough to make them effective. On the other hand some Assembly "recommendations" have in actual fact exerted far more influence than that term would normally lead one to expect. When a large number of nations, including the more influential ones, vigorously supported the Assembly Uniting for Peace resolution by a vote of 52 to 5 with 2 abstentions during the 1950 session, the recommendation carried tremendous weight.[58] On the other hand, during the same session when the Assembly adopted a resolution reaffirming a previous decision to internationalize

---

[58] Official Records of the Fifth Session ... Supplement No. 20, Resolutions, 19 September to 15 December 1950, p. 10.

Jerusalem, with a weak majority of only 38 to 14 with 7 abstentions and in opposition to the views of many of the more influential states, the decision was discredited from the very beginning.[59]

---

[59] Official Records of the Fourth Session ... Plenary Meetings, Summary Records of Meetings, 20 September-10 December 1949, p. 588.

III. INSTRUMENTS OF POLICY

When one examines the whole body of Assembly resolutions in the political field, one discerns certain types of action which the plenary body has developed as tools with which to achieve various substantive objectives. This chapter examines these tools while the next three deal with the substantive objectives themselves.

INVESTIGATION

One of the most useful functions that the Assembly performs is to assist in cutting away the jungle growth of rumor and confusion that usually surrounds every political issue. This is particularly important and yet particularly difficult in dealing with matters that approach the character of disputes in which the facts are not generally known and the heat of controversy distorts everyone's vision. The substitution of a multilateral for a unilateral investigation cannot eliminate prejudice altogether, but it can balance one special interest against another. The end result therefore is more likely to express an objective point of view than is an inquiry of more limited participation. The importance which the Assembly attaches to the results of these investigations is indicated by the reference which is frequently made to them in subsequent resolutions as the bases of the final substantive decisions. Thus the first sentence of the resolution adopted on 1 December 1950 regarding the Greek question began, "Having considered the unanimous conclusions of the United Nations Special Committee on the Balkans...."[1]

Use of Subsidiary Agencies

The organization of such investigations varies of course according to the circumstances of individual situations. The simplest form of inquiry is that in which the Assembly neces-

[1] Official Records of the Fifth Session of the General Assembly, Supplement No. 20, Resolutions, 19 September to 15 December 1950, p. 14.

sarily engages when it debates any issue in the process of arriving at a conclusion. Regarding many questions, however, the task of piecing the relevant facts together requires both time and travel which the entire Assembly membership cannot possibly devote to any single issue. In these instances the usual procedure has been to assign the investigatory function to *ad hoc* subsidiary agencies that can operate as extensively and continuously as the problem requires. Bodies of this character were established to study the questions regarding Greece, Palestine, Korea and Eritrea. More sedentary *ad hoc* committees have been established to work at headquarters between sessions studying organizational questions such as membership, Assembly methods and procedures, and the United Nations Field Service.

The Assembly has also organized certain standing bodies whose mandates include the authority to investigate any problems which may arise within the political sphere rather than only one particular situation. The first major body of this kind to be established was the Interim Committee, approved by the Assembly in November 1947, which was directed

... to consider and report ... to the General Assembly on any dispute or any situation which ... has been proposed for inclusion in the agenda ... or brought before the General Assembly by the Security Council ... to conduct investigations and appoint commissions of enquiry within the scope of its duties.[2]

Thus far, however, the Interim Committee has undertaken no investigatory activities.

Another standing body is the Peace Observation Commission, organized to implement the Uniting for Peace resolution adopted during the Assembly's 1950 regular session, which is now available, under the direction of the Assembly, the Interim Committee or the Security Council, to "observe and report on the situation in any area where there exists international tension the continuance of which is likely to

---

2 Official Records of the Second Session of the General Assembly, Resolutions, 16 September - 29 November 1947, pp. 15-16.

endanger the maintenance of international peace and security."[3]

Another standing committee with inquiry functions in the political field is the Special Committee which was established by the 1949 regular Assembly session for a three-year period to study and report to the plenary body on the information regarding non-self-governing territories which is submitted in accordance with Article 73 (e) of the Charter.[4] To initiate studies and formulate recommendations regarding the development of international law in implementation of Article 13 (1a) of the Charter, the 1947 regular session of the Assembly authorized the establishment of a permanent International Law Commission.

Whenever the Assembly organizes one of these bodies to conduct investigations it must struggle with the complex problem of what interests should be represented on them. Although many observers are convinced that agencies engaged in pacific settlement should be kept as small as possible, the task of investigation is generally considered to require relatively large groups. First, this allows the major interests within the Assembly to be included in the subsidiary bodies with the result that these interests are more likely to have a receptive attitude regarding the subsequent findings. Second, a large membership can facilitate the task of gathering information by dividing the burden into convenient segments. There are of course limits beyond which the size of these bodies should not be increased in the interest of efficiency. The number of members appointed to typical Assembly commissions has varied as follows: the United Nations Special Committee on Palestine, eleven; the United Nations Special Committee on the Balkans, eleven; the United Nations Temporary Commission on Korea, nine; and the Peace Observation Commission, fourteen.

---

3 Official Records of the Fifth Session ... Resolutions ... pp. 10-11.

4 For discussion of this and the preceding committees, see "International Responsibility for Colonial Peoples," *International Conciliation*, No. 458 (February, 1950), pp. 80-86.

In determining what kinds of interests are to be given special consideration in organizing these investigations, various criteria have been used. Probably the most common factor has been that of so-called "geographic distribution" which was mentioned specifically in connection with the establishment of the United Nations Special Committee on Palestine, the United Nations Special Committee on the Balkans and the Palestine Commission. The most frequent argument in support of this criterion is that to create a miniature Assembly is the very best way of assuring that the decisions of such a body will be shaped in accordance with the pattern of interests of the parent organ.

A second consideration has been the particular interests of the great powers, usually referred to in Assembly resolutions as the "permanent members of the Security Council." They were expressly included in the membership of the Special Committee on the Balkans because it was felt that no settlement would be realistic without the participation of the major powers, especially the United States and the Soviet Union, though as a matter of fact the Soviet Union later refused to take part in the work of the Committee. On the other hand they were expressly excluded from a Special Committee on Palestine and the Palestine Commission on the ground that their presence would hinder rather than facilitate the missions of those two groups. Obviously whether or not the great powers should be represented on such bodies cannot be decided by any rigid formula but must be determined in relation to the particular political environment of the moment.

A third criterion has been the special interests of certain limited groups of countries. On the United Nations Temporary Commission on Korea there was a heavy representation of countries located in the Pacific area: Australia, China, India and the Philippines. At other times states with special local interests have been specifically omitted as in the case of the Special Committee on Palestine.

Whether the members of such subsidiary bodies should be appointed as individuals or as the representatives of states has also been an important consideration. It has occasionally been suggested that an inquiry would be more objective if it were conducted by individuals appointed as private experts rather than as governmental delegates.[5] The more frequent attitude, however, especially on the part of the larger states, has been to urge governmental status for persons appointed to United Nations missions because individuals in that position are better able to speak with authority and to make decisions which are likely to win governmental support. This argument seems especially valid in the sensitive political field in which governments are loath to have "free-lancers" dealing with potentially explosive matters. The Assembly may of course stipulate special criteria which it wishes to have observed in the selection of individuals.

An even more important problem, the significance of which can scarcely be over-emphasized, is the caliber of the persons appointed to Assembly commissions. Unfortunately governments have occasionally selected individuals who have been so inadequate that they have seriously handicapped the work of such bodies. This is especially true of countries that do not have adequate, trained personnel resources for even their own internal needs. Such difficulties make it important that countries be impressed with the necessity of appointing only the most competent individuals to such posts. Because of this problem special pressures were brought to bear upon the countries that were named to appoint persons to the United Nations Commission for the Unification and Rehabilitation of Korea urging them to be particularly conscientious in making their selections. It is also hoped that the establishment of the "Panel for Inquiry and Conciliation," which the Assembly authorized in April 1949, will

---

[5] See Belgian suggestion to this effect regarding proposed commission on Jerusalem, Official Records of the Fifth Session ... *Ad Hoc* Political Committee, Summary Records of Meetings, 30 September - 14 December 1950, p. 518.

encourage governments to make available particularly well-qualified individuals.[6]

Use of Other Principal Organs

Besides establishing its own agents to conduct inquiries the Assembly has also discovered that the other United Nations principal organs can be useful instruments for gathering information and formulating related recommendations. As one might expect, the Security Council has been of central importance in this respect. Regarding the questions of Greece, Spain, Korea and Palestine which have been dealt with by the Council as well as the Assembly, the latter has found the Council's deliberations a rich source of useful background material. On the broader problem of arms regulation the Assembly has specifically requested the Council to study certain issues and report its findings to the Assembly. In general, however, the General Assembly, unlike the League Assembly, has not looked to the Council as the source of most of its information on specific situations and disputes but has preferred to organize such investigations under its own direct supervision.

In the trusteeship area the Charter itself provided that the Trusteeship Council should be the principal means of keeping the Assembly informed regarding that sphere of activity. The inquiries of the Trusteeship Council have been a most important device for reminding the administering states at regular intervals that the entire membership of the Assembly is looking over their shoulders.

The Economic and Social Council has also been utilized by the Assembly as a source of information and specific recommendations regarding the development of particular areas such as Korea, the former Italian Colonies and non-self-governing territories in general. Since it is obvious that economic and social factors are involved in every situation with which the Assembly has been concerned, it is to be

---

[6] Official Records of the Third Session of the General Assembly, Part II, 5 April-18 May 1949, Resolutions, p. 13.

expected that the Economic and Social Council will play an ever-increasing role in helping the plenary body to relieve specific as well as general tensions. The potential impact of such efforts upon the world's political problems was emphasized by Secretary of State Dean Acheson in his opening address during the 1950 session:

We must carry on with our war against want even as we arm against aggression. . . . We have it in our power now . . . to transform the lives of millions of people, to take them out from under the specter of want, to give people everywhere new hope. . . . These efforts . . . can have a combined impact of exciting proportions. . . . The place to begin, I submit to the Assembly, is Korea. I suggest that the General Assembly should call upon the Economic and Social Council to set up a United Nations recovery force to harness this great collective effort. . . .[7]

Finally the Secretariat has been a most important channel available to the Assembly for gathering information. Although the Secretariat has been extremely cautious in preparing studies on political questions, it has on occasion produced useful compilations, notably in connection with the Palestine question. It would be a significant contribution if the Secretariat would prepare even more studies of this kind in the future. On the basis of its research the Secretariat also exerts considerable influence by means of its specific policy recommendations, not only in the dramatic form of the Secretary-General's annual report and other special statements, but also in countless day-to-day contacts between the members of the Secretariat and the personnel of the national delegations.

Evaluation

In evaluating this whole development one is impressed by the fact that the Assembly's use of its investigatory authority has been one of the most important aspects of its role in the political field. Although few of its inquiries have been suffi-

---

[7] Official Records of the Fifth Session . . . Plenary Meetings, Verbatim Record, pp. 26-27.

ciently extensive or intensive, particularly in the case of Eri
trea, what facts they have presented have been most useful
While these multilateral reports may have lost some sharp
ness of focus in the process of accommodating many differen
points of view, they have at the same time been commend
ably balanced and objective and have gained wide support
What is even more significant, these inquiries have in many
instances made the Assembly's influence felt on the spot ir
Greece, Korea, Palestine and Eritrea. While the Assembly'
agents have not been able to enter such areas as North Korea
Albania, Yugoslavia, Bulgaria, Hungary, Rumania and
China, their exposition of the facts regarding the situation
in which these areas have been involved has exerted a direct
and compelling influence. The best measure of the impact
of that pressure is the ferocity with which those regimes have
denounced the Assembly's investigations.

PACIFIC SETTLEMENT

Another major element in many Assembly activities re
garding the political field is the effort to persuade disputing
states to reconcile their differences through some form of
pacific settlement. Although the Charter contains no specific
directive authorizing the Assembly to recommend procedures
of pacific settlement or to engage in such procedures itself
the Members have generally assumed that Articles 10, 11, 13
and 14 provide such authority implicitly if not explicitly.

In performing these functions the Assembly has tended to
make no rigid distinctions among the traditional forms of
"good offices," "mediation" and "conciliation" but has used
these terms almost interchangeably. The most frequent for
mula in fact has been for the Assembly to say merely that it
desires to "assist" the parties to reach a settlement, pre
sumably by whatever means of negotiation seem most appro
priate in each instance. This was the phraseology used in
resolutions concerning the Greek and Palestine questions.[8]

---

8 Official Records of the Third Session of the General Assembly, Part I,
21 September-12 December 1948, Resolutions, pp. 18 and 21, respectively.

During the 1950 session the Assembly directed a Standing Committee on the repatriation of Greek children to "consult with" the interested parties in order to settle the matter.[9] In using such flexible language the Assembly has demonstrated commendable wisdom in giving its agents maximum freedom to make the most of their broad mandates.

Neither arbitration nor judicial settlement has ever been formally recommended by the Assembly for the adjustment of any situation brought to its attention. Nevertheless the settlement of the former Italian Colonies question was virtually an instance of arbitration since the states concerned, the four victorious powers, agreed in advance to accept the Assembly's recommendation as binding. The relative success of this device has led to certain suggestions for the extension of the procedure to such controversies as that regarding the status of Formosa. While such a solution has the twin virtues of simplicity and finality, it is rarely feasible because the parties involved can seldom be persuaded that the arbitration tribunal is sufficiently neutral or that they cannot gain greater benefits for themselves in some other way.

Use of Subsidiary Agencies

Much of the Assembly's pacific settlement activity takes place within its sessions with a maximum of flexibility and a minimum of formal machinery. As we have already noted above, the Assembly President, various committee officers, and the Secretary-General are frequently called upon, as in the Greek situation, to confer with the states concerned in an effort to heal their differences. When the task has been particularly complex, has required traveling to specific areas, and has called for activity between as well as during Assembly sessions, it has been assigned to subsidiary agents such as those established to deal with the situations in Greece, Palestine and Korea. These bodies have varied in size from the single Palestine Mediator to the United Nations Special Committee on the Balkans with eleven members.

---

9 Official Records of the Fifth Session ... Resolutions ... p. 15.

The Interim Committee is a standing body which is also available for pacific settlement duties, although in practice it has never performed any functions in this field. Another standing body which one might expect would be involved in pacific settlement is the Peace Observation Commission. During the debate regarding its creation, however, it was made clear that the Commission was to engage in observation alone and not in pacific settlement. Nevertheless it is obvious that investigation is closely related to the process of conciliation and that a body which has studied the facts of a situation is in an admirable position to be of assistance in settling the conflict. Thus one might expect that the Peace Observation Commission would inevitably play a larger role in the area of pacific settlement than was anticipated when it was established.

Use of Other Principal Organs

As in investigation, so in pacific settlement the General Assembly has sometimes worked with other United Nations principal organs. The only significant occasion when the Assembly collaborated with the Security Council in this respect was in connection with the Palestine question. In that instance the Assembly made its agents responsible to the Security Council as well as to itself and requested the Council to support these bodies in their efforts to achieve an adjustment of the situation. It was that support, moreover, particularly the two truce orders, which finally made it possible to negotiate the armistice agreements. In connection with the Indonesian question the Assembly did no more in its resolution adopted in the spring of 1949 than support the pacific settlement efforts of the Security Council. Then in the fall of 1949 the Assembly welcomed the Hague agreement and commended the Security Council for the part that it had played in the matter.

Another principal organ, the International Court of Justice, has not had any questions referred directly to it by the Assembly for judicial settlement, although it has been requested to deliver advisory opinions both on the matter of South West Africa and the alleged violation of human rights in Bulgaria, Hungary and Rumania. There has been, in fact, a certain tendency on the part of Member states to ignore the potentialities of judicial settlement. This became so apparent in 1947 that the Assembly adopted a resolution urging acceptance of the compulsory jurisdiction clause of the Court "with as few reservations as possible," pointing out the advantages of "inserting in conventions and treaties arbitration clauses . . . for the submission of disputes . . . to the International Court of Justice" and recommending "as a general rule that States should submit their legal disputes to the International Court of Justice."[10] Since this resolution, however, there has been no evidence of any significant change in attitude toward the Court. The Assembly might well give greater thought to encouraging increased use of the Court for the settlement of disputes. The practical difficulties that stand in the way are of course obvious enough, but the Assembly should never cease using its influence to build confidence in the judicial process to the full extent of its feasibility under present circumstances.

A third principal organ, the Secretariat, works with tireless energy in all Assembly bodies and at all levels to try to reduce various tensions among the delegations. This has been done formally, as when the Secretary-General was asked by the 1948 regular session to help mediate the Greek conflict, and informally, as when the Secretary-General provided an opportunity for useful exploratory conversations by inviting the delegates of the Central People's Government of the People's Republic of China to his house during the 1950 session to dine with representatives of certain middle and small powers. Because of the Secretariat's central and continuing activities, its assistance is invaluable to the Assembly in matters of pacific settlement as in other fields.

---

10 Official Records of the Second Session of the General Assembly, Resolutions, 16 September-29 November 1947, p. 104.

Evaluation

The most important fact which emerges from this experience is that the General Assembly has considered pacific settlement as one of its foremost constructive functions. And it has played its role of peace-maker with a high degree of adaptability and a minimum of rigid formality. In spite of occasional criticisms that the Assembly is too unwieldy a body to engage in peaceful settlement, it has proved itself capable, particularly in the Palestine situation, of creating extremely effective agencies. Most observers who have considered the experience of these agents seem to agree that the peculiar requirements of the process of pacific settlement call for a body which can act with speed, flexibility and unity. Thus the Palestine Mediator is generally considered to have been a more appropriate instrument from this point of view than the larger and less flexible Special Committee on the Balkans.

The Assembly's experience thus far suggests that the intimate knowledge which any field commission is certain to gather regarding a particular situation places it in a most advantageous position, not only for pacific settlement, but also for specific substantive recommendations. In actual practice these functions are inevitably related and tend to reinforce each other. It is essential in the adjustment of any conflict to keep formulating persuasive alternatives for presentation to the right people at the right time. Messrs. Bernadotte and Bunche were especially adept at this art. In a general progress report submitted in September 1948, the Mediator demonstrated his shrewd appreciation of the political and military factors involved. "He considered that after each side had had an unpleasant taste of bitter fighting and had had a three months 'cooling-off period of relative calm' during the two truces, the time was ripe for a settlement."[11] His appraisal of the complementary roles of the

---

[11] The United Nations Mediator (and Acting Mediator) for Palestine, Memorandum prepared for the Interim Committee, 1950, p. 56.

Assembly and Security Council, as indicated in the following passage of his progress report, is especially interesting:

> I am reasonably confident that, given the permanent injunction against military action issued by the Security Council, and firm political decisions by the General Assembly, both sides will acquiesce, however reluctantly, in any reasonable settlement on which is placed the stamp of the approval of the United Nations.... What is indispensable is that the General Assembly take a firm position on the political aspects of the problem ... and that its resolution be so reasonable as to discourage any attempt to thwart it and to defy the Security Council order by the employment of armed force.[12]

POLICY RECOMMENDATIONS

Specific Disputes and Situations

Besides engaging in inquiries and pacific settlement efforts the General Assembly has also frequently declared its own views on the substantive issues of particular political problems. This raises the question of when and to what extent the Assembly should adopt specific recommendations as a means of facilitating a settlement. It seems obvious that the principal task of the Assembly is to harmonize conflicting views rather than to impose a decision contrary to those views. Yet at times pressure may be necessary in order to break a deadlock. It was exactly this kind of pressure which finally produced wide if not unanimous agreement on the disposition of the former Italian Colonies. Thus in almost all cases the Assembly has combined some specific substantive recommendations together with some form of pacific settlement. The recommendations may be very broad and general as in many of the resolutions on the Greek question, or they may be more detailed as in the Palestine and Italian Colonies resolutions.

In formulating such policy statements the Assembly often relies heavily upon the advice of the subsidiary agencies and

---

[12] *Ibid.*, pp. 57-58.

other United Nations organs that have been discussed above. In the Palestine question, for example, the United Nations Special Committee on Palestine furnished the general outline of the partition plan which was finally adopted by the Assembly. Both Messrs. Bernadotte and Bunche, the Palestine Mediator and Acting Mediator respectively, were particularly enterprising in bringing their views on substantive issues to the attention of the Assembly. Count Bernadotte succeeded on his own initiative in having the Palestine question placed on the agenda of the first part of the third session in the fall of 1948 in order to suggest certain modifications of the original partition plan which he hoped might provide the basis for a settlement. In connection with the Assembly's settlement of the Italian Colonies question, the Trusteeship Council was requested to formulate a draft trusteeship agreement for Somaliland, to include a special guarantee of the rights of individuals; the agreement worked out by the Council was approved by the Assembly in its 1950 session. The Interim Committee was empowered to make recommendations concerning two issues — the future status of Eritrea and the question of threats to the political independence and territorial integrity of China and to the peace of the Far East — though actually it failed to make any distinct contribution to the settlement of either.

Formal resolutions drafted by the Assembly are sometimes not enough, however, to produce an effective solution. Frequently the most useful details are those filled in on the spot by an Assembly agent, such as the Commissioner in Libya, operating within the broad framework of the Assembly's instructions. In some cases the Assembly has given other organs considerable leeway in the formulation of such details. The United Nations Temporary Commission on Korea was authorized to consult with the Interim Committee if it needed advice concerning the supervision of elections in Korea. When the Commission was refused permission to enter North Korea, it accordingly turned to the Interim Committee, which, in an historic decision with far-reaching repercussions, directed it to go ahead even if its activities were limited to South Korea. As part of the 1947 resolution recommending the partition of Palestine, the Assembly gave the Trusteeship Council a mandate to adopt a detailed Statute for Jerusalem along lines outlined by the Assembly.

General Political Questions

In addition to the Assembly's recommendations on specific disputes and situations there have also been substantive recommendations regarding general political questions affecting the entire United Nations membership. The most important of these that are touched upon in this study are the resolutions regarding armaments regulation, various "peace" plans and the progressive development of international law. In these matters also the Assembly has occasionally sought advice from other principal organs as well as its own subsidiary bodies: the Security Council in connection with armaments regulation, and the International Law Commission regarding international law development. Although the Assembly was given no specific Charter authority to formulate conventions in the political field it has actually spent what some observers feel is an inordinate amount of time in the consideration of such draft conventions as those dealing with genocide and the Nürnberg principles. In this connection there is a growing belief that the Assembly could and should make better use of other bodies of more limited and expert membership for the detailed drafting of such conventions and restrict its own functions to general approval or disapproval.

Evaluation

The function of formulating substantive recommendations in the name of the entire United Nations membership is a significant step beyond mere inquiries or even pacific settlement. It is a clear recognition that international political questions affect the whole community as well as those directly involved and that decisions regarding such questions should take into account the views of the total community. In this manner, resolution by resolution, a foundation is being built which may ultimately be the groundwork for a true international government.

PROMOTION OF COMPLIANCE

The final and crucial ingredient in any Assembly resolution is the element that is added to dissolve resistance and promote compliance. Although every text book underlines the fact that such resolutions are not legally binding the Assembly constantly strives to make them as effective in practice as if they were binding. Although it has suffered great disappointments in these efforts it has at the same time managed to win far more cooperation in some instances than most observers thought possible.

Formal Recommendations

The first means of promoting compliance which the Assembly has utilized is the very instrument of a formal recommendation in the name of the United Nations. Members are frequently reminded that they assumed certain solemn obligations with respect to such recommendations when they ratified the United Nations Charter, including paragraphs 2, 3 and 5 of Article 2:

2. All Members, in order to ensure to all of them the rights and benefits resulting from membership, shall fulfil in good faith the obligations assumed by them in accordance with the present Charter.

3. All Members shall settle their international disputes by peaceful means in such a manner that international peace and security, and justice, are not endangered.

5. All Members shall give the United Nations every assistance in any action it takes in accordance with the present Charter, and shall refrain from giving assistance to any state against which the United Nations is taking preventive or enforcement action.

Furthermore, as indicated in the discussion on voting, an Assembly resolution adopted by a large and influential majority carries great weight which no country, regardless of its size, finds easy to oppose.

Several means have been used to give additional force to such resolutions. One method is to seek advance commitments to comply with certain kinds of recommendations. The decision of the four great powers to accept the Assembly's recommendations on the former Italian Colonies was the first formal use of this device. It has also been suggested in connection with settling questions regarding membership, Spain and Formosa, but without success. The Uniting for Peace resolution makes use of this procedure by soliciting advance indications by the Members as to the military contingents and other resources they are willing to set aside for use in accordance with Assembly or Security Council recommendations. Since any attempt to make Assembly resolutions binding in all instances is patently visionary at this time, this device of advance pledges of compliance on certain limited questions is a most useful and promising development.

Surveillance

The General Assembly has also taken advantage of the restraining influence of international surveillance as another means of promoting compliance. As Philip Jessup has put it, the United Nations is an instrument for "mobilizing world public opinion and making it articulate to the point at which it becomes a factor in the power situation."[13] One form of this sanction is the "watchdog" function which the Assembly's agents in Korea, Greece and Palestine have performed to good advantage. Thus the 1949 mandate of the United Nations Commission on Korea included a directive to "observe and report any developments which might lead

---

13 Philip Jessup, "The U. N. Begins to Show Power Against Power," *The New York Times Magazine*, 23 October 1949, p. 12.

to or otherwise involve military conflict in Korea."[14] A similar, though less direct, version of the watchdog function was provided for in the 1950 resolution regarding the observance of human rights and fundamental freedoms in Bulgaria, Hungary and Rumania:

> *The General Assembly ... invites* Members of the United Nations, and in particular those which are parties to the Treaties of Peace with Bulgaria, Hungary and Rumania, to submit to the Secretary-General all evidence which they now hold or which may become available in future in relation to this question; *likewise invites* the Secretary-General to notify the Members ... of any information he may receive in connexion with this question.[15]

Another form of this instrument of collective surveillance is the Assembly's use of various field agents to supervise the carrying out of particular recommendations or agreements. The Special Committee on the Balkans was directed to "observe the compliance by the four Governments concerned with the foregoing recommendations [and] ... to be available to assist the four Governments concerned in the implementation of such recommendations."[16] A more specific mandate was issued to the Commission on Korea in the fall of 1948 to "observe the actual withdrawal of the occupying forces and verify the fact of the withdrawal when such has occurred...."[17] The Palestine Mediator and later the Conciliation Commission were both given the responsibility by the Security Council, in keeping with the Assembly's general instructions, of supervising various truce and armistice agreements in Palestine. In all three of these instances the fact that the Assembly has had its own eyes and ears at the scene of the difficulty has exerted an important controlling influence that should not be under-estimated merely because it

---

14 Official Records of the Fourth Session of the General Assembly, Resolutions, 20 September-10 December 1949, p. 15.

15 Official Records of the Fifth Session ... Resolutions ... p. 16.

16 Official Records of the Second Session ... Resolutions ... p. 13.

17 Official Records of the Third Session ... Part I ... Resolutions, p. 26.

has not always been supported by economic or military pressure.

An area in which the Assembly has used strong and continuing pressures to promote compliance has been in the administration of territories in which the Assembly has been especially interested. In Libya and Korea, for example, the Assembly has stationed agents to assist in preparing those areas for independent self-government. In the case of the trust territories the Assembly has given general direction to the efforts of the Trusteeship Council in supervising the governing of those areas. To bring special pressure to bear upon the Union of South Africa with respect to South West Africa the Assembly passed a resolution during its 1950 session establishing

a Committee of five ... to confer with the Union of South Africa concerning the procedural measures necessary for implementing the advisory opinion of the International Court of Justice and to submit a report ... to the next regular session ...; to examine the report on the administration of the Territory ... covering the period since the last report, as well as petitions and any other matters relating to the Territory ..., and to submit a report thereon....[18]

To exercise its authority with respect to all other non-self-governing territories the Assembly operates through its Special Committee on Information Transmitted under Article 73e of the Charter.

It should also be said in this connection that the Secretariat plays a central role in implementing all Assembly recommendations. At the end of each session the Secretariat carefully studies its own special responsibilities with regard to each resolution and outlines appropriate courses of action. Thus the Secretariat's continuing interest in winning as high a degree of collaboration as possible on the part of all of the Members is an important part of the total compliance effort.

---

[18] Official Records of the Fifth Session ... Resolutions ... p. 56.

Sanctions

Finally the General Assembly has, on a few occasions, attempted to organize diplomatic, economic and military measures as means of gaining compliance with its recommendations or with what it considers the basic postulates of the Charter. The only instance of the Assembly's use of direct and formal diplomatic sanctions was in the resolution regarding Spain which was adopted in the fall of 1946 recommending that the "Franco Government of Spain be debarred from membership in international agencies established by or brought into relationship with the United Nations" and that "all Members of the United Nations immediately recall from Madrid their Ambassadors and Ministers plenipotentiary accredited here."[19] This resolution itself was only a recommendation, of course, implementation of which depended on the individual will of each Member. It has been suggested that offending non-member states such as Bulgaria, Hungary, Rumania and Albania might be threatened with a refusal to admit them to membership until they have complied with the wishes of the United Nations, but such a suggestion has not yet been adopted.

An interesting effort to mobilize collective political pressure to carry out an Assembly recommendation was the Assembly's 1948 directive to the Trusteeship Council concerning the internationalization of Jerusalem. Reiterating its previous determination to internationalize the city, the Assembly requested the Trusteeship Council to "complete the preparation of the Statute of Jerusalem . . . and proceed immediately with its implementation."[20] The resolution provided further that the Council "shall not allow any actions taken by any interested Government or Governments to divert it from adopting and implementing the Statute of Jerusalem." Since both Israel and Jordan — the two states occupying the city — had declared their uncompromising

---

19 Resolutions Adopted by the General Assembly During the Second Part of Its First Session From 23 October to 15 December 1946, p. 64.
20 Official Records of the Fourth Session . . . Resolutions . . . p. 25.

opposition to the plan, it could obviously be implemented only by force. The Trusteeship Council declined to undertake this task, however, and merely referred the problem back to the Assembly.[21]

The Assembly authorized resort to economic pressure when it passed a resolution during its 1949 session requesting all Members as well as other states

to refrain from any action designed to assist . . . any armed group fighting against Greece; to refrain from the . . . provision of arms or other materials of war to Albania and Bulgaria until the Special Committee or another competent United Nations organ has determined that the unlawful assistance of these States to the Greek guerrillas has ceased.[22]

No effort was made, however, to organize any collective implementation of this recommendation. During the 1946 and subsequent debates on the Spanish question, several suggestions for economic sanctions were proposed, including the French plan to boycott food shipments from Spain and the Byelorussian suggestion to stop all trade and communications with Spain. In view of frequent protests by the Soviet bloc against strengthening the Assembly in the political field it is interesting to note that this group has consistently urged that the Assembly authorize economic, as well as diplomatic, sanctions against Spain.

The first really determined application of economic sanctions came as a result of the deliberations of the special committee established on 1 February 1951 to investigate additional measures to be used against the aggressors in Korea. Thus on 18 May 1951 the Assembly recommended that

every state: (a) apply an embargo on the shipment to areas under the control of the Central People's Government of the People's Republic of China and of the North Korean authorities of arms, ammunition and implements of war, atomic energy

[21] Official Records of the Fifth Session, Supplement No. 9, Question of an International Régime for the Jerusalem Area and Protection of the Holy Places: Report of the Trusteeship Council.

[22] Official Records of the Fourth Session . . . Resolutions . . . p. 9.

materials, petroleum, transportation materials of strategic value, and items useful in the production of arms, ammunition and implements of war; (b) determine which commodities exported from its territory fall within the embargo, and apply controls to give effect to the embargo; (c) prevent . . . the circumvention of controls on shipments applied by other states pursuant to the present resolution. . . .[23]

With this resolution the Assembly banned a wider range of materials than the League had attempted to control in connection with the Italo-Ethiopian conflict, though it was not yet willing to establish the kind of collective supervisory machinery which the League had created immediately to check on compliance.

The Assembly first recommended the possible use of force to support a resolution in the 1947 Palestine recommendation which requested the Security Council to "determine as a threat to the peace, breach of the peace or act of aggression, in accordance with Article 39 of the Charter, any attempt to alter by force the settlement envisaged by [that] resolution."[24] When the Palestine Commission informed the Security Council in February 1948 that attempts were being made to prevent by force implementation of the plan and asked for the Council's aid,[25] the Security Council did not accept the theory that one of its functions was to enforce political decisions of the Assembly. Warren Austin led the way by stating that

The Charter of the United Nations does not empower the Security Council to enforce a political settlement whether it is pursuant to a recommendation of the General Assembly or of the Security Council itself.

. . . The Security Council, under the Charter, can take action to prevent aggression against Palestine from outside. . . . But this action must be directed solely to the maintenance of international peace. The Security Council's action, in other words, is directed to keeping the peace and not to enforcing partition.[26]

---

23 United Nations Doc. A/1805, 21 May 1951.
24 Official Records of the Second Session . . . Resolutions . . . p. 132.
25 United Nations Doc. S/676, 16 February 1948.
26 United Nations Doc. S/PV.253, 24 February 1948, p. 48.

The Council's subsequent action in bringing hostilities to an end made no mention of the partition plan.

Under the new Uniting for Peace resolution, the Assembly now has at hand a strong weapon for implementing its recommendations, at least insofar as they relate to the maintenance of international peace and security. Section C of the resolution

Recommends to the States Members of the United Nations that each Member maintain within its national armed forces elements so trained, organized and equipped that they could promptly be made available ... for service as a United Nations unit or units, *upon recommendation by the Security Council or the General Assembly.* [italics added][27]

Prior to the adoption of the Uniting for Peace resolution the Assembly had already, on 7 October 1950, assumed the authority to issue directives relating to military matters within the scope of action of the United Nations Command set up by the Security Council in June to repel the aggression from North Korea. Later, on 1 February 1951, after the item had been removed from the Security Council agenda, the Assembly made further recommendations regarding the collective security effort in Korea.

Evaluation

From this experience, it is clear that the Assembly is moving ever closer toward providing "teeth" for its recommendations. There is now scarcely any limit to the means which the Assembly can employ if it chooses. The only important limitation is that the Assembly may make only recommendations, not binding decisions of the kind that the Security Council may use under Chapter VII. Thus the effectiveness of the Assembly's efforts depends on the degree of the Members' compliance in each case. This fact makes it all the more essential that the Assembly act responsibly and adopt only those measures which have the support of a large and influential majority.

---

[27] Official Records of the Fifth Session ... Resolutions ... p. 11.

IV. MAJOR DECISIONS ON SPECIFIC SITUATIONS

It is not surprising that the Assembly has found itself at the very center of the international squalls which have buffeted the world during the past five years. It would have been not only surprising but disappointing if the Assembly had descended into a storm cellar and isolated itself from those forces. Having discussed above the various instrumentalities which have been available to the plenary body for its use in coping with the political issues that have challenged it, it is perhaps appropriate to review briefly the substantive highlights of the major decisions that have been made in the three categories of problems mentioned before: (1) situations affecting limited sectors of the international community, (2) general problems affecting the entire community, and (3) organizational problems related to the political field.

The most dramatic and most publicized aspect of the Assembly's role in the political sphere has been its efforts with respect to the first category: to extinguish certain political fires that have burst forth in various disturbed areas. At the outset one should realize that the General Assembly has become more directly and deeply involved in this kind of activity earlier in its existence than its predecessor, the League Assembly. The General Assembly has dealt with nine situations plus the continuing problems of trusteeship and other non-self-governing territories during its first five years, while the League Assembly dealt directly with no disputes during its first eleven years and with only four during the rest of its existence.[1] Nor did the latter have any direct responsibility with respect to the Mandates System. Among

---

[1] Margaret E. Burton, *The Assembly of the League of Nations* (Chicago, University of Chicago Press, 1941), Chapters IX and X. The four disputes were the Sino-Japanese, Bolivia-Paraguay, Finno-Russian, and Italo-Ethiopian questions.

the various factors that are responsible for this difference between the activities of the two Assemblies certainly the most obvious is the rift between the Soviet and non-Soviet worlds which has so restricted the functions of the Security Council. Another element is the fact that the League Assembly's cautious development in the sphere of specific disputes established a precedent which has strengthened the role of the General Assembly.

As one reviews the work of the General Assembly it is also important to note that the fundamental issues which lie at the root of the problems which have confronted it have been the same issues that are primarily responsible for the tensions afflicting the world as a whole today: the East-West conflict and the restless discontent that is prevalent among various underprivileged peoples. The Assembly's decisions regarding the problems that have grown out of these issues can be grouped roughly for purposes of this analysis into three principal objectives which the Assembly has sought to achieve: (1) to promote the observance of international obligations regarding certain fundamental rights and freedoms, (2) to stimulate the creation of new political orders, and (3) to prevent aggressive intervention.

Fundamental Rights and Freedoms

The Assembly's principal efforts to enforce certain international obligations regarding fundamental human rights have been the actions it has taken with respect to the Franco government in Spain, the treatment of Indians in South Africa and the alleged violations of fundamental freedoms in Bulgaria, Hungary and Rumania.

Spanish Question

The Spanish question was raised during the first part of the Assembly's first session in February 1946 by the "left wing" of the Assembly, including the Soviet group, strongly supported by many other countries that had so recently suffered at the hands of the Nazis and their allies. The resolution which they succeeded in having approved reaffirmed a San Francisco resolution and a declaration made during the Potsdam Conference which stated that Spain under the Franco government was not qualified for United Nations membership.[2] In April 1946 Poland, backed by the Soviet Union, asked the Security Council to direct Members to sever diplomatic relations with Spain. Failing in this attempt, these two countries persuaded the Council to remove the matter from its agenda so that the Assembly might deal with the issue. Despite considerable resistance, especially on the part of the United States and the United Kingdom to the suggestions for an economic boycott, the final compromise resolution adopted at the second part of the first session was still surprisingly ambitious. It recommended that the specialized agencies debar the Franco government from membership, that all United Nations Members withdraw their top-ranking diplomatic officers from Spain and that the Security Council consider other measures to be taken if a government representative of the Spanish people were not established within a reasonable time.[3]

Although later statements by the Franco government indicated that it was disturbed by this resolution it gave no indication of being prepared to make any concessions. The Assembly action was of course not as extreme as it seemed on the surface, since forty-nine of the fifty-five Members had no ambassadors or ministers plenipotentiary accredited to Spain at the time the resolution was adopted. Of the others only Argentina expressly refused to comply. When the Assembly convened for its second regular session at the end of 1947 the non-interventionist forces were gathering strength and argued that the character of the Franco regime was a domestic question within the meaning of Article 2 (7) of the Charter. Thus the Assembly did no more than express

---

[2] Resolutions Adopted by the General Assembly During the First Part of Its First Session From 10 January to 14 February 1946, p. 39.

[3] Resolutions Adopted by the General Assembly During the Second Part of Its First Session From 23 October to 15 December 1946, pp. 63-64.

"its confidence that the Security Council will exercise its responsibilities under the Charter as soon as it considers that the situation . . . so requires."[4]

The growing non-interventionist sentiment prevented the plenary body from adopting any of several suggested resolutions during the second part of the third session in the spring of 1949 and from even discussing the matter during the fourth session at the end of that year. Finally during the 1950 session the balance of opinion had shifted so far that the Assembly decided to retreat to the extent of revoking the recommendation for the withdrawal of ambassadors and ministers and the debarring of Spain from membership in "agencies established by or brought into relationship with the United Nations."[5]

Indians in the Union of South Africa

The General Assembly first considered the question of the treatment of Indians in South Africa during the second part of the first session in the fall of 1946 when the Indian government charged that the racial policies of the Union of South Africa were violations of both the United Nations Charter and certain bilateral commitments. South Africa replied that the Charter provisions did not specifically prohibit the South African actions and furthermore that the whole question was within that country's "domestic jurisdiction." In spite of this opposition the Indians, strongly supported by Asian countries and other sympathetic delegations, won a substantial victory when the Assembly adopted a resolution stating

that the treatment of Indians in the Union should be in conformity with the . . . agreements concluded between the two Governments and the relevant provisions of the Charter . . . [and that] the two Governments [were] to report at the next session . . . the measures adopted to this effect.[6]

---

[4] Official Records of the Second Session of the General Assembly, Resolutions, 16 September-29 November 1947, pp. 21-22.
[5] Official Records of the Fifth Session of the General Assembly, Supplement No. 20, Resolutions, 19 September to 15 December 1950, p. 17.
[6] Resolutions . . . Second Part . . . First Session . . . p. 69.

When the Assembly met for its second session in the fall of 1947, India announced that the situation had grown worse rather than better and persuaded the First Committee to adopt a draft resolution reaffirming the 1946 recommendation and suggesting that the two parties engage in a round-table discussion to be based on that recommendation. This draft resolution failed however to win a two-thirds majority in plenary meeting largely because the United States, the United Kingdom and others believed that the 1946 resolution had been unwise and were unwilling to reaffirm it. During the second part of the third session in the spring of 1949 a French-Mexican draft proposing a round-table conference without mentioning the 1946 resolution was finally adopted.[7] The situation grew steadily worse, however, especially with the passage of the South African Group Areas Act, and India called for action once more at the Assembly's 1950 session. After a thorough review of the problem the Assembly adopted a new resolution by the rather weak majority of 33 in favor, 6 against and 21 abstaining. Its provisions recommended that

the Governments of India, Pakistan, and the Union ... proceed ... with the holding of a round table conference ... ; that, in the event of failure ... there shall be established for the purpose of assisting the parties ... a commission of three members, one ... to be nominated by the ... Union ..., another ... by ... India and Pakistan and the third ... by the other two members or ... by the Secretary-General ... .[8]

Bulgaria, Hungary and Rumania

The question of the alleged violation of human rights in Bulgaria and Hungary was first raised during the second part of the third session in the spring of 1949 as a protest against the recent trials of Joseph Cardinal Mindszenty of Hungary and fifteen pastors of Protestant churches in Bulgaria. The Soviet Union and certain other states insisted

7 Official Records of the Third Session of the General Assembly, Part II, 5 April-18 May 1949, Resolutions, p. 6.
8 Official Records of the Fifth Session ...Resolutions ... p. 24.

that the matter was one that lay within the "domestic jurisdiction" of the states concerned and thus was not subject
to United Nations intervention. Finally on 29 April the
Assembly cautiously expressed

its deep concern at the grave accusations made against the [two]
Governments . . . ; [noted] with satisfaction that steps have been
taken by several States signatories to the Peace Treaties with
Bulgaria and Hungary regarding these accusations, and expresses
the hope that measures will be diligently applied . . . .[9]

When these countries and Rumania failed to demonstrate
any willingness to modify their policies, the Assembly during
its fourth session at the end of 1949 adopted, in preference
to an Australian proposal for the appointment of an Assembly commission of inquiry, a United States-sponsored resolution submitting the following questions to the International
Court of Justice for its advisory opinion:

"1. Do the diplomatic exchanges between Bulgaria, Hungary
    and Rumania on the one hand and certain Allied and
    Associated Powers . . . on the other . . . disclose disputes sub-
    ject to the provisions . . . of the Treaty . . . with Bulgaria,
    . . . the Treaty . . . with Hungary, and . . . the Treaty . . . with
    Rumania?"
"2. Are . . . Bulgaria, Hungary and Rumania obligated to . . .
    [appoint] their representatives to the Treaty Commissions?"
"3. If one party fails to appoint a representative . . . is the Secre-
    tary-General of the United Nations authorized to appoint
    the third member of the Commission upon the request of
    the other party to a dispute . . . ?"
"4. Would a Treaty Commission composed of a representative
    of one party and a third member appointed by the Secretary-
    General . . . constitute a Commission . . . competent to make
    a definitive and binding decision in settlement of a dis-
    pute?"[10]

On 30 March 1950 the Court delivered its answers to the
first two questions and on 18 July 1950, the answer to the
third: (1) the disagreements do constitute a dispute within

---

[9] Official Records of the Third Session . . . Part II . . . Resolutions, pp. 17-18.
[10] Official Records of the Fourth Session of the General Assembly, Resolutions, 20 September-10 December 1949, pp. 16-17.

the meaning of the peace treaties; (2) the Balkan states concerned are obligated to observe all the terms of those treaties; (3) if one party should fail to appoint a representative, however, the Secretary-General may not appoint a third member on the request of the other party; (4) in view of the third answer the Court did not reply to the fourth question.[11] This decision was no surprise to most of the members nor did it present any magic formula for settling the matter. When the Assembly convened for its fifth session at the end of 1950 the large majority of the members did not see how they could do more than condemn

the wilful refusal of the [three] Governments . . . to fulfil their obligation . . . to appoint representatives to the Treaty Commissions . . . [and invite] Members . . . to submit to the Secretary-General all evidence which they now hold or which may become available in future in relation to this question . . . [and invite] the Secretary-General to notify the Members . . . of any information he may receive in connexion with this question.[12]

Evaluation

Any appraisal of these efforts to promote the observance of fundamental human rights should take into account the fact that the Assembly has had no easy or direct access to the areas of tension. Four of the five countries involved are not Members of the United Nations and none of them has allowed any kind of direct United Nations intervention. In spite of these barriers most of the Members have been anxious to make vigorous use of the Assembly's limited powers.

As for the Assembly's use of its various instrumentalities, in none of these cases did it engage in any very thorough investigation of the relevant facts although this would seem to be one of the most constructive contributions that it could make. In the Spanish situation it was content to use the material provided by the Security Council; in the Balkan situation it asked the Secretary-General only to receive and

---

11 United Nations Doc. A/1348, 13 September 1950.
12 Official Records of the Fifth Session . . . Resolutions . . . p. 16.

disseminate information that may be submitted by the Members and did not even take this step until recently; in the South African question it has not sought to gather any additional information.

In general one can say that the Assembly's efforts in these instances were a serious challenge to the regimes concerned and gave sustaining hope to their critics. On the other hand the Assembly's actions produced no startling results and in some cases gave rise to increased oppression. This is of course the reaction to external pressure that is to be expected from such regimes. It should not discourage the Assembly from criticizing oppression but it should be a warning to that body not to attempt the impossible. If the Assembly over-reaches itself, it creates frustration in its own house and causes a reaction in the opposite direction. Nothing can have a more demoralizing effect upon the whole organization.

In addition to these efforts to deal with specific violations of fundamental rights and freedoms, the Assembly has also contributed to the development of and adherence to positive standards of human rights in various parts of the world. The Assembly's Korean Commission worked out an elaborate and extremely valuable set of criteria to safeguard freedom of elections, insisted on procedures consonant with these criteria and supervised their execution. In Greece the Assembly has attempted to promote political freedom; in Palestine it has been concerned with religious freedom; and in the various trust and non-self-governing territories it has recently laid particular stress upon freedom of education. Especially notable is the model trusteeship agreement for Italian Somaliland with its annexed "Declaration of Constitutional Principles" which specifies the political, legal, economic and social rights which must be respected by the Administering Authority.

CREATION OF NEW POLITICAL ORDERS

The second major Assembly objective related to specific areas has been its efforts to foster peaceful change. These have ranged from blueprinting the evolution of non-self-governing territories into statehood to promoting the progressive advancement of dependent and underdeveloped areas. In three cases—Palestine, Korea and the Italian Colonies—the Assembly has adopted resolutions for the purpose of creating new political and social orders.

Palestine

The Palestine question was first referred to the Assembly by the United Kingdom in April 1947 under Article 10 of the Charter as a request for preliminary study leading to recommendations "concerning the future government of Palestine."[13] The Assembly then convened for its first special session to deal with the almost insoluble problem which had been created by the Balfour Declaration. In 1917 Lord Balfour had promised the Jews "a national home" in Palestine and at the same time had added, without prejudice to "the civil and religious rights of existing non-Jewish communities." Between this time and 1947, the Jewish population of Palestine rose from 56,000 to 608,000 and Arab and Jewish villages had become hopelessly intermingled. Growing Jewish aspirations for statehood had been driven to a pitch of frenzy by the Nazi atrocities, while Arabs inside and outside of Palestine watched with anger and alarm the intrusion into their barren homeland of a powerful alien element with far superior financial resources and technical skills. The Mandatory Power was in the unhappy position of trying to mediate between two irreconcilable forces and to redeem an inherently contradictory pledge.

Although there had been a number of previous commissions of inquiry during the many vain efforts to cut the Gordian knot, the Assembly decided to send a Special Committee on Palestine to make its own examination on the spot and report to the second session. By the fall of that year a majority of the members of the Special Committee had decided to recommend the partition of Palestine into a Jewish and an Arab state, harnessed together by a United Nations-

---

13 United Nations Doc. A/286, 3 April 1947.

supervised economic union. In spite of intense Arab opposition to this plan, the Assembly, influenced primarily by the views of the United States and the Soviet Union, adopted a partition plan which followed the general outline of the Special Committee's recommendation. A United Nations Commission was to be established which would gradually assume administrative authority from the United Kingdom in preparation for the termination of the Mandate not later than 1 August 1948. At the same time the Commission would assist the Arab and Jewish communities to create their respective governments. It was also proposed that the two governments accept an agreement that would provide for mutual economic and social cooperation, including the protection of certain religious and minority rights.[14] Although this resolution was legally no more than a "recommendation," the Assembly inserted passages which were intended to promote compliance, as mentioned above, and which leaned heavily on the Security Council's authority under Chapter VII of the Charter.

The Commission, however, never had an opportunity to do more than acquire the label of the "five lonely pilgrims" since the Jews and Arabs soon began to resort to violence. After the United Kingdom announced in January that it would consider the Mandate terminated on 15 May 1948, the fighting began to grow more intense.

The Commission then turned to the Security Council for assistance, declaring that "powerful Arab interests . . . are defying the resolution of the General Assembly and are engaged in a deliberate effort to alter by force the settlement envisaged therein."[15] The Security Council, however, as noted above, demonstrated a distinct reluctance to assume responsibility for implementing political decisions of the Assembly, although it later intervened to stop hostilities, and on 1 April threw the problem back at the General Assembly by calling that body into special session. When the General Assembly

---

[14] Official Records of the Second Session . . . Resolutions . . . pp. 131ff.
[15] United Nations Doc. S/676, 16 February 1948, p. 3.

met on 16 April 1948 the United States submitted a proposal for trusteeship to replace the partition plan. Most of the members, however, were reluctant to re-examine the partition resolution or to try to impose a trusteeship plan. The final compromise was to appoint a Mediator with the brief but staggering mandate to "promote a peaceful adjustment of the future situation of Palestine."[16] By brilliant improvisation and shrewd utilization of a Security Council truce resolution of 29 May 1948 the Mediator was able to achieve a temporary cessation of hostilities and to begin his mediation efforts. As the first truce came to an end without any real settlement and the fighting broke out again, the Mediator called for new Security Council action. Thus the Council on 15 July 1948 invoked Chapter VII for the first time by finding that "the situation in Palestine constitutes a threat to the peace within the meaning of Article 39 of the Charter."[17] In the same resolution the Council went on to order the governments concerned to "desist from further military action," an order which was soon put into effect.

After further fruitless negotiations the Mediator asked the Assembly to place the matter on the agenda for its third session and proposed a plan of his own calling for a more stable peace and certain adjustments in the provisions of the original partition resolution of 29 November 1947.[18] Unhappily Count Bernadotte's invaluable efforts were brought to a sudden end by his tragic assassination on 17 September 1948. Fortunately his able assistant, Ralph Bunche, was ready to take his place as Acting Mediator. Dr. Bunche discovered, however, when the Assembly met for its third session on 21 September that there was strong resistance to any tampering with the original resolution. Finally it was decided in accordance with Count Bernadotte's proposal to appoint a Conciliation Commission to "assume, in so far as it considers necessary in existing circumstances,

---

16 Official Records of the Second Special Session of the General Assembly, Supplement No. 2, Resolutions, 16 April-14 May 1948, p. 5.
17 United Nations Doc. S/902, 15 July 1948.
18 United Nations Doc. A/648, 18 September 1948.

the functions given to the United Nations Mediator . . . ; [and] to carry out the specific functions and directives given to it . . . by the General Assembly or by the Security Council. . . ."[19] Nevertheless, the Acting Mediator remained in the field for eight more months negotiating armistice agreements. After tireless prodding by the Acting Mediator, supported by several Security Council resolutions, these negotiations were initiated on 12 January 1949, and after the most complex and delicate discussions the armistice agreements were completed the following summer and their administration was entrusted to mixed commissions headed by United Nations observers. Unfortunately, however, there has been little progress since that time in the matter of achieving a permanent peace settlement.

The special problem of protecting the holy sites in Jerusalem has been a particularly difficult aspect of the Palestine question because of the various religious and political interests involved. Certain Catholic and Arab (other than Jordan) groups, together with the Soviet bloc, have urged thorough internationalization along the lines of the provisions of the original partition resolution: that the "City of Jerusalem shall be established as a *corpus separatum* under a special international regime and shall be administered by the United Nations."[20]

Jordan and Israel have consistently opposed internationalization while many other states have tried to formulate some middle position between the two extremes.

When fighting broke out in the spring of 1948 and the second special session was called, the Assembly recommended that the United Kingdom appoint a neutral acceptable to both sides to serve as Special Municipal Commissioner in Jerusalem.[21] That plan failed however when the man appointed, Harold Evans, a United States Quaker, arrived in Jerusalem only to find that the Arabs would not cooperate.

---

[19] Official Records of the Third Session of the General Assembly, Part I, Resolutions, 21 September-12 December 1948, p. 22.

[20] Official Records of the Second Session . . . Resolutions . . . p. 146.

[21] Official Records of the Second Special Session . . . Resolutions . . . p. 7.

Then the Mediator assumed responsibility for Jerusalem as part of the entire Palestine problem. In the fall of 1948 the Assembly asked the Conciliation Commission to prepare a new statute for a permanent international regime in Jerusalem. The plan that was presented by the Commission during the fourth session at the end of 1949 recognized the existing division of the city between Israel and Jordan and recommended that the international regime be limited to the Holy Places. Despite warnings that internationalization had become a practical impossibility, the Assembly decided to reaffirm the original project of a permanent international regime and instructed the Trusteeship Council, as has been noted above, to formulate and implement such a plan without delay.[22] But when the members gathered for the Assembly's fifth session in 1950 they were confronted with the plain fact that the Trusteeship Council was unable to comply with its instructions. After lengthy debate a Belgian resolution was adopted by the First Committee calling for a new study, but the proposal failed to win a two-thirds majority in plenary meeting.

Another difficult aspect of the Palestine problem with which the Assembly has concerned itself has been the problem of the 950,000 Arab refugees who fled from Palestine during the conflict. Wisely the Assembly has recognized the direct relationship between this issue and the total Palestine situation and has accepted the responsibility of seeking a just and practicable solution of the problem. In response to the Mediator's recommendations, the Assembly resolved in December 1948: (1) that refugees wishing to return home and live at peace should be permitted to do so at the earliest practicable date, with compensation for those not wishing to do so; (2) that the newly-formed Conciliation Commission should facilitate repatriation, resettlement and economic and social rehabilitation of the refugees;[23] and (3) that a Director for United Nations Relief for Palestine Refugees be ap-

---

22 Official Records of the Fourth Session ... Resolutions ... p. 25.
23 Official Records of the Third Session ... Part I ... Resolutions, p. 21.

pointed by the Secretary-General and be supported by voluntary governmental contributions which it was suggested should approximate $32,000,000.[24]

When it became apparent that immediate repatriation was impossible and that far more complex and long-range positive efforts would be required, the Conciliation Commission authorized an Economic Survey Mission, under the direction of Gordon Clapp, Chairman of the Board of the Tennessee Valley Authority, to study the situation. On the basis of the Mission's report the Assembly, on 8 December 1949, established a United Nations Relief and Works Agency for Palestine Refugees in the Near East to administer a program of relief and public works again to be financed by voluntary contributions in the estimated amount of $54,900,000.[25]

Finally, when the Assembly met for its fifth session it recommended: (1) that both direct relief and the work program should be continued, (2) that governments which had not made any contributions should make every effort to do so, (3) that the "reintegration," by either repatriation or resettlement, of the refugees should be facilitated, and that a total of $50,000,000 should be contributed for these various purposes.[26] Yet in spite of all of these efforts the Assembly's Palestine refugee program is still seriously blocked by a combination of three stubborn factors: Israel's refusal to admit more than a token handful of refugees; Arab opposition to any substantial resettlement; and the reluctance of most United Nations Members to make any very generous offers of assistance.

Korea

In the other two instances in which the Assembly has created a new political order, it has inherited problems involving World War II settlements. These cases are especially

24 *Ibid.*, p. 66.
25 Official Records of the Fourth Session ... Resolutions ... p. 23.
26 Official Records of the Fifth Session ... Resolutions ... p. 22.

interesting because there was strong feeling at the San Francisco Conference that the United Nations should not become involved in settling the issues of the war but should begin with a clean slate.[27] One of the factors behind this attitude was the memory that the League was intimately involved in the peace settlements of World War I and that this fact had given rise to bitter criticism, particularly in the United States.

The "problem of the independence of Korea" was brought to the attention of the Assembly during the second session in the fall of 1947 by the United States after that country had failed to arrive at a settlement with the Soviet Union in accordance with the Moscow Agreement of December 1945. The Soviet spokesmen vigorously opposed this move on the ground that it violated not only certain commitments between the Soviet Union and the United States but also Article 107 of the Charter which provides that

Nothing in the present Charter shall invalidate or preclude action, in relation to any state which during the Second World War has been an enemy of any signatory to the present Charter, taken or authorized as a result of that war by the Governments having responsibility for such action.

Most of the other members were unhappy to see such an explosive issue forced upon the Assembly at such an early stage in its career. At the same time many of them agreed with the United States that the open sore of Korea should be healed as soon as possible and that in view of the impasse between the two occupying powers it was perhaps better for the United States to act through the United Nations than to proceed unilaterally.

While the Palestine case involved a conflict of interest within the area, the Korean situation was primarily a problem of a dispute between two alien powers. For thirty years the former Kingdom of Korea had been occupied by the Japanese. As the second World War drew to a close, by

---

27 Herbert V. Evatt, *Task of Nations* (New York, Duell, Sloan and Pearce, 1949), Ch. VII.

mutual agreement the Soviet Union forces moved into that part of Korea north of the thirty-eighth parallel while the United States forces took the southern part. This occupation was to serve a dual purpose: first to accept the surrender of the Japanese forces; and second, to supervise the establishment of Korea as an independent democratic state, in consultation with the Korean democratic parties and organizations. Negotiations between the two occupying powers broke down over the definition of "democratic."

The problem facing the Assembly was to achieve in practical terms a definition which would not only meet the criteria implicit and explicit in the Charter but which would also be acceptable to the occupying powers.

Over the protests of the Soviet Union, the General Assembly, in November 1947, created the Temporary Commission on Korea, which was to supervise the election of Korean representatives and to ensure that such an election should be held under conditions permitting full and free participation of the Korean people.

After the Temporary Commission was established it soon became obvious that the Soviet Union would not cooperate and that it would be impossible to hold elections north of the thirty-eighth parallel. The Commission then decided to return to the Interim Committee for further instructions and some of the Commission's members, including Chairman Menon of India, confidently expected that it would be decided not to hold elections limited to the southern part of the country. But the Interim Committee was persuaded to accept the United States thesis that half a democracy is better than none at all. Thus elections on that basis were held in May 1948 under conditions which the Commission finally decided provided a "free," but far from ideal, atmosphere.

During its third session in the fall of 1948 the Assembly declared that

there has been established a lawful government (the Government of the Republic of Korea) having effective control and jurisdiction over that part of Korea where the Temporary Commission was able to observe and consult and in which the great majority of the people of all Korea reside ... and that this is the only such Government in Korea; ... that the occupying Powers should withdraw their occupation forces from Korea as early as practicable; ... that, as a means to the full accomplishment of the objectives set forth in the resolution of 14 November 1947, a Commission on Korea ... shall be established to continue the work of the Temporary Commission ... to: (a) lend its good offices to bring about the unification of Korea ... (b) seek to facilitate the removal of barriers ... (c) be available for observation and consultation in the further development of representative government based on the freely-expressed will of the people....[28]

When the Assembly met for its fourth session a northern Democratic People's Republic of Korea had been set up north of the thirty-eighth parallel under the premiership of Kim Il Sung, revolutionary Communist leader. The two governments—north and south—faced each other in an atmosphere of mounting tension. There was little that the Assembly could do but extend the mandate of its watchdog commission and instruct it to be on the alert for any signs of overt hostilities.

On 25 June 1950 the dam burst with the North Korean attack which gave rise to the immediate organization of collective forces under the direction of the Security Council —with the Soviet delegate absent—to resist the aggression. During five weeks of debate and decision by the Council, the Assembly had effective support in defending from aggression the new state it had sponsored, but a different situation arose when the representative of the Soviet Union returned to the Council in August. No longer could the Council be counted upon to take effective leadership in dealing with hostilities which showed no signs of abating. When the Assembly convened on 19 September the Korean situation was the first item to be considered by the First Committee. The military situation was paramount in the minds of the delegates and the Assembly's final omnibus resolution carried

---

[28] Official Records of the Third Session ... Part I ... Resolutions, pp. 25-26.

specific recommendations to the United Nations Command with regard to the reestablishment of order in Korea.[29] The Assembly declared that "all constituent acts be taken ... for the establishment of a unified, independent, and democratic government in the sovereign State of Korea" and stipulated that "United Nations forces should not remain in any part of Korea otherwise than so far as necessary for achieving the objectives specified...."[30] Finally, the resolution provided that

a Commission ... to be known as the United Nations Commission for the Unification and Rehabilitation of Korea be established to assume the functions hitherto exercised by the present ... Commission on Korea; represent the United Nations in bringing about the establishment of a unified, independent and democratic government of all Korea; exercise such responsibilities in connexion with relief and rehabilitation in Korea as may be determined by the General Assembly after receiving the recommendations of the Economic and Social Council.

One particularly significant aspect of this resolution is its recognition of the direct influence of economic and social conditions upon political conditions.

The greatest challenge came, however, when the forces of the People's Republic of China intervened in Korea early in November. After an interval in which the Security Council endeavored in vain to arrive at some agreed course of action, the Assembly attempted through a Good Offices Committee to negotiate a cease-fire. When no results had been obtained after six weeks, the question came up for reconsideration.

The United States insisted that the Chinese People's Republic should be condemned for its aggression, while an Arab-Asian group led by India urged that the emphasis be placed on negotiation rather than condemnation. Finally on 1 February 1951 the Assembly accepted the United States position, condemned the People's Republic of China as an

---

29 For further details see p. 138.
30 Official Records of the Fifth Session ... Resolutions ... p. 9.

aggressor, and urged that a committee composed of the members of the Collective Measures Committee consider additional measures. On 7 May the United States presented to that committee a comprehensive economic warfare plan which, after it had been considerably softened particularly at the behest of the United Kingdom and France, became the committee's first report to the Assembly. The resolution, adopted in plenary meeting on 18 May, provided, as noted above, that every state should apply and enforce individually, rather than collectively, an embargo on various categories of war materials.[31]

Italian Colonies

Though the problem of the Italian Colonies came to the Assembly because of the failure of the Big Four to arrive at a settlement, as provided for in the Italian Peace Treaty, it did not constitute a major source of friction between any of the great powers. Neither were there within the area any strong forces in opposition to each other. The "collection of deserts," Libya, Eritrea and Italian Somaliland, was of strategic interest but of no economic value. A four-power commission sent out in 1947 by the Deputies of the Council of Foreign Ministers found that all three colonies were intensely poor, with no prospect of being economically self-sustaining in the future, and that none of them was politically, socially, or educationally sufficiently developed at the present time to form and maintain an effective national government.

Such was the problem which faced the General Assembly. Though the issue came to it during the first part of its third session in September 1948, discussion was postponed until the second part of the session the following spring in order to give the members additional time to study the matter. When that time arrived the debate centered about the conservative approach of the United Kingdom and the United States, which were both concerned with safeguarding their

---

[31] United Nations Doc. A/1805, 21 May 1951.

strategic interests in the Middle East, and France, which feared any move which might cause unrest in her neighboring colonies; the Soviet Union which was unsuccessful in obtaining a foothold as an administering authority and favored direct United Nations administration or independence; the Latin American states which tended to favor Italy's interests; and the Arab states which opposed Italy's return to the territories and wanted early independence for the Arab populations concerned.

The representatives of the inhabitants, who received rather a full hearing, did little to facilitate a solution. The only common basis of agreement was a strong repugnance to a return of Italian administration in any form. Internal divisions, both political and religious, and lack of political organization and sophistication resulted in a fragmentation of views and opinions.

Because it was impossible to discover an adequate compromise formula during that session the decision was postponed until the fourth session to be held in the fall of 1949. At that time, with Italian-United Kingdom negotiations setting the pace, the Assembly was finally able to agree on an acceptable arrangement which provided that

A. *With respect to Libya* ... that Libya ... shall be constituted an independent and sovereign State; that this independence shall become effective as soon as possible and in any case not later than 1 January 1952; that, for the purpose of assisting the people of Libya in the formulation of the constitution and the establishment of an independent Government, there shall be a United Nations Commissioner in Libya appointed by the General Assembly and a Council to aid and advise him ...

B. *With respect to Italian Somaliland* ... that Italian Somaliland shall be an independent sovereign state; that this independence shall become effective at the end of ten years from the date of the approval of a Trusteeship Agreement by the General Assembly; that, during the period mentioned ... , Italian Somaliland shall be placed under the International Trusteeship System with Italy as the Administering Authority ... aided and advised by an Advisory Council ...

C. *With respect to Eritrea* . . . that a Commission consisting of representatives of not more than five Member States, as follows, Burma, Guatemala, Norway, Pakistan and the Union of South Africa, shall be established to . . . examine the question of the disposal of Eritrea and to prepare a report for the General Assembly. . . . The Interim Committee . . . shall consider the report and proposal . . . of the Commission and report, with conclusions, to the fifth regular session of the General Assembly. . . .[32]

When the Commission on Eritrea returned from its mission its five members were split into three different factions. Burma and South Africa wanted Eritrea to be a self-governing unit federated with Ethiopia under the crown of the latter. Norway proposed that Eritrea be reunited with Ethiopia except for the western province to be left provisionally under United Kingdom administration. Guatemala and Pakistan insisted that Eritrea should be placed under a direct ten-year United Nations-administered trusteeship after which time it would become independent.[33] This report then went to the Interim Committee which was able to do very little with it except to serve as the forum in which certain conversations were initiated by the United States and the United Kingdom that ultimately produced an acceptable resolution. Its provisions, which were adopted by the Assembly during its fifth session, recommended that

Eritrea shall constitute an autonomous unit federated with Ethiopia under the sovereignty of the Ethiopian Crown . . . There shall be a transition period which shall not extend beyond 15 September 1952, during which the Eritrean Government will be organized and the Eritrean Constitution prepared and put into effect . . . During the transition period, the present administering Power shall continue to conduct the affairs of Eritrea. It shall, in consultation with the United Nations Commissioner, prepare as rapidly as possible the organization of an Eritrean administration . . . The United Nations Commissioner shall, in consultation with the administering Power, the Government of

---

[32] Official Records of the Fourth Session . . . Resolutions . . . pp. 9-12.

[33] Official Records of the Fifth Session of the General Assembly, Supplement No. 8, Report of the United Nations Commission for Eritrea.

Ethiopia, and the inhabitants of Eritrea, prepare a draft of the Eritrean Constitution to be submitted to the Eritrean Assembly and shall advise and assist the Eritrean Assembly in its consideration of the Constitution.[34]

During the fifth session the report of the Commissioner for Libya was also considered by the Assembly. The discussion demonstrated unfortunately how difficult it is for an entire main committee such as the *Ad Hoc* Political Committee, composed as it is of many persons who are inadequately informed regarding the complex issues involved, to give proper direction to the efforts of a field agent. Nevertheless, after a spirited tug-of-war among the various interests, the Assembly was able to agree on a resolution that followed the general pattern of the Commissioner's own recommendations:

that a National Assembly duly representative of the inhabitants of Libya shall be convened as early as possible, and in any case before 1 January 1951; that this National Assembly shall establish a Provisional Government of Libya as early as possible, bearing in mind 1 April 1951 as the target date; that powers shall be progressively transferred to the Provisional Government by the administering Powers in a manner which will ensure that all powers at present exercised by them shall, by 1 January 1952, have been transferred to the duly constituted Libyan Government.[35]

Evaluation

As we look back over this experience, it becomes evident that the Assembly has accomplished something very significant in these three difficult situations — Palestine, Korea and the Italian Colonies. It has dared to walk into these troubled areas, tense with nationalist sentiment and vulnerable to extremist movements, and has played a leading role in actually establishing new political regimes which have gone a long way toward satisfying the aspirations of the major groups involved. Although the Assembly cannot be given

---

[34] Official Records of the Fifth Session ... Resolutions ... pp. 20-21.
[35] *Ibid.*, p. 17.

all of the credit in any of these cases, it has been one of the principal factors in channeling and directing these revolutionary forces so as to avoid a political inundation that might engulf the entire world. In these efforts it has gone far beyond anything which the League Assembly was ever able to achieve. While it is true that the General Assembly's activities in these matters have affected only territories which were not self-ruling, this experience may well lead to the utilization of the Assembly in the future to deal with situations concerning independent territories. To appreciate the full impact of these efforts one must evaluate them one by one.

In the Palestine situation the Assembly proved to be a most useful instrument not only for producing a thorough investigation of the situation but also for formulating a partition plan that had the support of the great majority of Members including the United States and the Soviet Union. While this plan was altered by military force, largely in favor of Israel, its general outlines greatly influenced the thinking of all parties concerned; they provided a strong political and psychological weapon for the Israelis; and they have actually been implemented to a substantial degree. Regarding its pacific settlement function the Assembly made no progress in the early stages of the situation, but the Mediator did an admirable job of supervising the various truce and armistice negotiations. Although the Assembly made no attempt to apply any sanctions directly, it did create the agencies, principally the Mediator, which were largely responsible for establishing and maintaining the armistices. While the Security Council refused to accept the Assembly recommendation to use the former's authority under Chapter VII to enforce the partition plan, it did virtually the same thing by giving its support to the Mediator and by invoking Chapter VII finally to halt the fighting after partition had been accomplished by force of arms. At present the primary needs are to tie more closely together the various agencies concerned with the Palestine problem — the Conciliation Commission, the Truce Supervision Organization and the Relief and Works Agency for Palestine Refugees — and to bring increasing pressure to bear upon the parties to persuade them to agree upon a final peace settlement.

In the Korean situation the Assembly initiated no investigation of its own before making its 1947 recommendation that elections be held to prepare for the establishment of a Korean national government. Since that time, however, the various Assembly commissions which have gone to that country have performed the valuable function of giving the United Nations and the world at large a relatively objective multilateral account of what has actually been taking place in that unhappy peninsula. While the Assembly and its agents have tried many times to persuade the parties to engage in pacific settlement negotiations, the Russians and North Koreans have steadfastly refused to cooperate. In formulating the plan to make Korea independent some of the Assembly members feared that too much was being attempted too quickly, but they were finally persuaded to accept the United States point of view. To judge the wisdom of this decision one must consider the alternatives that were available. There was no readiness whatever on the part of the Koreans to accept any form of trusteeship. Nor did it seem wise to force the United States to act unilaterally outside the United Nations when it had been criticized for doing so in connection with the Truman Doctrine. Nor was the United States prepared to allow the matter to continue to smolder without doing something positive about it. Thus the Assembly seems to have chosen the most feasible course of action.

With respect to implementing the 1947 independence plan, the Assembly sent its agents to the spot and did a relatively good job in spite of the many obstacles. With the outbreak of North Korean and Chinese aggression, however, the problem of implementation has grown more complex. At present the Assembly has four heads watching the Korean situation: the Commission for the Unification and Rehabilitation of Korea, the Good Offices Committee, the Additional Measures Committee and the Korean Reconstruction Agency. At the same time the Unified Command in Korea, which was organized by the United States in accordance with a Security Council recommendation of July 1950 and which has received directives from both the Council and the Assembly, receives no regular supervision from either organ. Regarding this latter military problem it has been suggested that an Assembly Korean Military Staff Committee, composed of the nations which are contributing the military forces, be established to provide collective and regular supervision of the Unified Command. Beyond this it would also seem appropriate at this time to coordinate more fully the activities of all of the various bodies that have a finger in the Korean pie. One means of doing this would be to recast the Commission for the Unification and Rehabilitation of Korea in order to make it representative of the major interested countries, including those that are contributing armed forces, so that it might serve as the principal nerve center.

Regarding the Italian Colonies the Assembly undertook no field investigation except for the rather hasty survey of the Eritrean situation. It depended primarily on the somewhat conflicting findings of the four-power investigation, previously carried out under the authority of the Council of Foreign Ministers, and the highly-charged testimony delivered at Lake Success by the representatives of various interested groups. As for pacific settlement, this case is the first time that the Assembly has been authorized to deliver an arbitral decision accepted in advance by the parties. Fortunately the Assembly rose to the occasion after considerable maneuvering and produced plans which received strong support, including that of the United States and the United Kingdom. As one student of the problem has put it,

the General Assembly's second effort [November 1949] resulted in an acceptable solution to what had so long been an unsolvable problem. Although the resolution was by no means entirely satisfactory to everyone concerned, it is worth noting that, except for the lone negative vote of Ethiopia, opposition was recorded merely in the form of abstentions.

The key to the success of the fourth session's resolution lay in its satisfying both the anti-colonial and the pro-Italian blocs with something less than each had been ready to settle for at the third session.[36]

The Eritrean decision in the 1950 session was less successful, with ten opposing votes, including those of the Soviet bloc, as well as four abstentions. With respect to implementation the task was made relatively easy by the advance agreement among the great powers. At the same time the agencies which the Assembly has created have exerted considerable influence in preparing these areas for self-rule. On the other hand the experience thus far indicates that a main committee such as the *Ad Hoc* Political Committee is an unwieldy instrument for guiding the work of an agent like the Commissioner for Libya. A special sub-committee would undoubtedly be a more effective body for this kind of function.

Thus the Assembly has met the challenge of some of the most complex and explosive questions that have confronted the United Nations. And it has gone far beyond mere tinkering; it has overhauled whole regimes and created new political orders. No development of the Assembly's role in the political field is more significant than this.

Indonesia

In one further instance of the coming into being of a new state, the Assembly's role was a very minor one. The Indonesian question was placed on the Assembly's agenda during the second part of the third session in the spring of 1949, at the behest of India and Australia, in order to indicate the Assembly's concern regarding that situation, even though there was general agreement that the Security Council should continue to have primary responsibility for dealing with the matter. It was decided to postpone considera-

---

[36] Benjamin Rivlin, *Italian Colonies*, United Nations Action 1 (New York, Carnegie Endowment for International Peace, 1950), p. 61.

tion of the item, however, until the fourth session when it was learned that the parties to the dispute had announced that they were prepared to negotiate a settlement. Then, while the Assembly was meeting for its fourth session, the parties arrived at an agreement at the Hague and the plenary organ was content to adopt a resolution commending everyone, including the Security Council, for the successful negotiations.[37]

Underprivileged Peoples

Less dramatic but equally revolutionary in their long-range implications have been the Assembly's efforts to bring the underprivileged peoples closer to partnership in the world community. Though the Expanded Programme for Technical Assistance was handled in the Assembly purely as an economic question, its political ramifications are too far-reaching to avoid mention in the present study. Countries numbed by poverty and ignorance are being helped to climb the long ladder of progress. Countries which have been dependent upon foreign skills, capital and interests for the exploitation of their natural resources are learning to develop their own potentialities. Countries cut off from the world, without railroads, planes or other means of communication, are being brought into relationship with other nations.

While the program for technical assistance covers both states and dependent territories, the Assembly has a special responsibility for the latter. In accordance with Chapter XII of the Charter, eleven trust agreements, including the most recent one concerning former Italian Somaliland, have been approved by the Trusteeship Council and the Assembly, and both of these organs have worked hard to make United Nations supervision of the administration of those areas more than a pious hope. Because of the strength of the anti-colonial forces in the Assembly a great deal of pressure, some of it unreasonable but most of it constructive, has been

---

37 Official Records of the Fourth Session ... Resolutions ... p. 23.

brought to bear upon the administering powers in the interests of the dependent peoples.

One of the unresolved issues related to trust areas is the status of the former mandated territory of South West Africa, the only former League mandate which has not either been placed under the Trusteeship System or given independence.

In 1946 the General Assembly recommended that the territory be placed under trusteeship and invited the Union to propose a trusteeship agreement. The Union replied only that it would administer the territory in the spirit of the mandate and would submit reports on its administration for the information of the United Nations. A report was duly submitted.

In 1947 the General Assembly reaffirmed its resolution of the previous year, asking the Union to place the territory under trusteeship, and authorized the Trusteeship Council in the meantime to examine the report.

In 1948 the General Assembly once again considered the question, in view of the Union's non-compliance. The representative of the Union argued that "there was no legal obligation" and "no moral obligation"[38] requiring the Union to place South West Africa under trusteeship. Nevertheless, the Assembly adopted a resolution regretting the failure of the Union to comply with its requests, repeating its recommendation that South West Africa be placed under trusteeship and, furthermore, recommending that the Union continue to submit annual reports until the future of the territory was decided.

The Union government made clear its resentment of the criticism it had received in the United Nations and its intention of pursuing a unilateral course. In July 1949 it informed the United Nations that it could "no longer see that any real benefit is to be derived from the submission of special reports on South West Africa to the United Nations,

---

[38] Official Records of the Third Session of the General Assembly, Part I, Plenary Meetings, Summary Records of Meetings, 21 September-12 December 1948, p. 585.

and ... in the interests of efficient administration,"[39] they would no longer be forwarded. At the same time the Union transmitted a copy of a legislative act providing for "certain changes" in the relationship between the Union and South West Africa, which in effect brought them into closer association.

Faced with this intransigence, the Assembly decided to reiterate its previous recommendations and also to submit certain legal questions to the International Court.[40] The Court's opinion, delivered on 11 July 1950, declared in essence that South Africa is not competent to modify the status of South West Africa unilaterally without the consent of the United Nations, that South Africa continues to be subject to the obligations laid down in Article 22 of the League Covenant and the terms of the original mandate, and that the function of supervising the administration of South West Africa should be exercised by the United Nations.[41] Taking its cue from this opinion the Assembly approved a new resolution during its fifth session requesting that South Africa continue to carry out the provisions of the original mandate, including the submission of petitions and annual reports, and establishing a committee of five to consult with the Union regarding implementation of the opinion of the Court and also to examine the report and petitions relating to South West Africa.[42]

Closely linked to the Assembly's responsibilities with respect to the Trusteeship System are its efforts to strengthen the United Nations influence in other non-self-governing territories according to the provisions of Chapter XI of the Charter. Out of the passages of that chapter has been fashioned a formidable instrument to use as a lever to improve the lot of the 200,000,000 people who still have not won self-government. The principal accomplishments in this direction have been the adoption by the Assembly of reso-

---

[39] United Nations Doc. A/929, 13 July 1949, pp. 2-3.
[40] Official Records of the Fourth Session ... Resolutions ... p. 45.
[41] United Nations Doc. A/1362, 15 September 1950.
[42] Official Records of the Fifth Session ... Resolutions ... p. 56.

lutions urging Members possessing dependent territories to submit information on political development, which is not specifically required by Chapter XI, as well as information on economic, social and educational conditions which is required; establishing the Special Committee to examine this information and make appropriate recommendations; and urging that greater attention be devoted to the economic and social needs of these territories in collaboration with the specialized agencies.[43]

Evaluation

It is of course no accident that these problems regarding non-self-governing territories have demanded so much of the Assembly's time and energies. One of the most powerful revolutionary forces of our day is the irrepressible awakening of great masses of people who have learned from the more developed nations the meaning of freedom as well as the usefulness of the material gadgets of western civilization. Because of the strong representation in the United Nations of states that were once dependent and thus place an understandably high value on independence, the Assembly has been exceptionally active in this field. Fortunately the international community has long been recognized as having certain supervisory responsibilities with respect to dependent peoples, and thus the Assembly is able to have more direct access to these problems than the promotion of the observance of fundamental freedoms within sovereign states. However, the case of South West Africa is a clear indication that the successful implementation of the Assembly's objectives in this field are also dependent upon the cooperation of the administering authorities.

PREVENTION OF AGGRESSIVE INTERVENTION

Another major objective which the Assembly has sought in dealing with certain specific situations has been to prevent

---

[43] See "International Responsibility for Colonial Peoples," *International Conciliation*, No. 458 (February, 1950).

aggressive intervention. This has been a primary consideration in the questions concerning Greece and China, which
will be discussed here, as well as Korea and Palestine.

Greece

The Greek case was first brought to the attention of the
Security Council in January 1946 by the Soviet Union in
protest against the presence of British troops in Greece, but
the Council took no action. When the issue was raised again
in August 1946 by the Ukrainian Soviet Socialist Republic
the United States suggested sending a commission of inquiry
to look into the matter, but the Soviet Union vetoed the
proposal. Then when Greece itself asked for United Nations
aid against external intervention, the members of the Security Council, including the Soviet Union, approved the
United States plan to send a Commission of Investigation
Concerning Greek Frontier Incidents. That Commission reported back in May 1947, accusing Albania, Bulgaria and
Yugoslavia of aiding Greek guerrillas, and recommending
that a commission of non-permanent members of the Council be appointed to assist in restoring peace. France abstained
in the finding of guilt while the Soviet Union and Poland
strongly opposed both the findings and recommendations of
the Commission. As a result of this impasse the Council was
able to do no more than remove the item from its agenda
so that it might be considered by the Assembly.

When the plenary organ met for its second regular session
in the fall of 1947 the United States, which was particularly
disturbed by the Security Council's failure to meet the challenge of the Greek situation, introduced as one of its major
proposals the substance of the Security Council Commission's findings and recommendations. The Soviet Union
produced a counter-proposal which was strikingly similar to
that of the United States in its use of the Assembly in this
matter: a finding of guilt (against Greece), a program of
pacific settlement, and a suggestion for the creation of an
Assembly agency to help implement the settlement. Out of

this conflict of views emerged a resolution, adopted on 21 October 1947, which called upon the four states concerned to

cooperate in the settlement of their disputes by peaceful means, . . . establish normal diplomatic . . . relations, . . . establish frontier conventions, . . . co-operate in the settlement of the problems arising out of the presence of refugees in the four States . . .; [and established] a Special Committee (1) to observe the compliance by the four Governments concerned with the foregoing recommendations, (2) to be available to assist the four Governments concerned in the implementation of such recommendations. . . .[44]

When the Assembly convened for its third session at the end of 1948 it had before it the Special Committee's report which indicated that the situation was as threatening as ever and recommended that the Assembly continue its efforts to promote a settlement. After a review of the entire situation a new resolution was adopted which extended the life of the Special Committee with much the same mandate that it had been given before.[45] By the time of the fourth session in the fall of 1949 serious weaknesses were beginning to appear among the aggressive forces ranged against Greece, due primarily to the defection of Yugoslavia and the aid provided by the United States. The Assembly decided, nevertheless, not to disband the Special Committee but to direct it to give special attention to the possibility of pacific settlement through the appointment and utilization of "the services and good offices of one or more persons whether or not members of the Special Committee."[46] It also, as mentioned above, requested all states to refrain from supplying Albania and Bulgaria with war materiel.

When the Assembly met for its fifth session in 1950, the conflict had eased so radically because of the factors mentioned above that the plenary body could refer in its resolution, approved on 1 December 1950, to "a certain improve-

---

[44] Official Records of the Fourth Session . . . Resolutions . . . p. 13.
[45] Official Records of the Third Session . . . Part I . . . Resolutions, p. 20.
[46] Official Records of the Fourth Session . . . Resolutions . . . p. 10.

ment . . . in the situation on the northern frontiers of Greece."[47] At the same time it recommended that the Special Committee continue to perform its various functions until the next session "unless meanwhile the Special Committee recommends to the Interim Committee its own dissolution."[48] The Assembly also requested the International Committee of the Red Cross and the League of Red Cross Societies to continue, as they had been doing for several years, to cooperate with the United Nations in promoting the repatriation of Greek soldiers and children.

China

The question of "threats to the political independence and territorial integrity of China and to the peace of the Far East resulting from Soviet violations of the Sino-Soviet Treaty of Friendship and Alliance of 14 August 1945 and from Soviet violations of the Charter of the United Nations" was first referred to the Assembly by the Chinese delegation during the fourth session in the fall of 1949. The Soviet group immediately protested that the matter should not be considered by the Assembly because the delegation that had submitted it did not have the right to speak for the Chinese people. Many other delegations were hesitant to commit the plenary body to any very vigorous action because of their uncertainty with respect to the final outcome of the struggle then going on in China. Finally the Assembly adopted two resolutions. A joint Australia-Mexico-Pakistan-Philippines-United States recommendation called upon all states to

respect the political independence of China, . . . to respect the right of the people of China . . . to choose freely their political institutions and to maintain a government independent of foreign control, to respect existing treaties relating to China, [and] to refrain from (a) seeking to acquire spheres of influence or to create foreign-controlled regimes . . . (b) seeking to obtain special rights . . . within the territory of China.[49]

---

47 Official Records of the Fifth Session . . . Resolutions . . . p. 14.
48 *Ibid.*
49 Official Records of the Fourth Session . . . Resolutions . . . p. 13.

A joint Cuba-Ecuador-Peru recommendation referred the item to the Interim Committee "for continuous examination and study . . . [and requested it to] report to the next regular session of the General Assembly with recommendations, or to bring it to the attention of the Secretary-General with a view to reporting to the Security Council if it deems necessary. . . ."[50]

The Interim Committee was, however, no more willing to take any positive steps in the matter than the Assembly had been, particularly in view of the Soviet bloc's campaign to boycott United Nations bodies that refused to unseat the Chinese Nationalist representatives. After gingerly avoiding the subject during most of the inter-session period, the Interim Committee finally agreed with the sentiments expressed by its chairman shortly before the convening of the Assembly's fifth session:

It is possible . . . that to debate the item . . . in the context of the present political situation would not serve a useful purpose. . . . I suggest that the Interim Committee would facilitate the work of the General Assembly if it were to decide not to debate this question. . . .[51]

Nevertheless, after the Assembly failed again during its fifth session to agree upon a positive course of action, it decided once more to "instruct the Interim Committee to continue inquiry on this question in order to obtain more information . . . and to report to the General Assembly. . . ."[52]

Korea and Palestine

It is also appropriate in connection with this discussion of the Assembly's efforts to prevent aggressive intervention to mention briefly the particular aspects of the Korean and Palestine questions that are related to this analysis. The fact that a United Nations commission was on the spot to report

---

[50] *Ibid.*, p. 14.
[51] Official Records of the Fifth Session of the General Assembly, Supplement No. 14, Report of the Interim Committee of the General Assembly, p. 3.
[52] Official Records of the Fifth Session . . . Resolutions . . . p. 15.

objectively and independently on the North Korean attack greatly facilitated — and was perhaps basic to — the swiftness with which the Security Council was able to reach agreement on a course of action. When the Assembly met for its fifth session, it recommended that "all appropriate steps be taken to ensure conditions of stability throughout Korea."[53] This provision was generally understood to be an implicit authorization for the United Nations Command to cross the thirty-eighth parallel. It is worth noting in this connection that the Security Council resolution of 25 June merely referred to the withdrawal of the armed forces of North Korea to the thirty-eighth parallel.[54]

After the People's Republic of China intervened, the Assembly adopted another resolution on 14 December 1950 requesting the President of the General Assembly

to constitute a group of three persons, including himself, to determine the basis on which a satisfactory cease-fire in Korea can be arranged and to make recommendations to the General Assembly as soon as possible.[55]

On 11 January the Cease-Fire Group, which had previously reported to the First Committee its inability to make satisfactory arrangements for a cease-fire, submitted to the Committee a supplementary report covering five basic principles essential to a settlement of the Korean situation.[56] The principles dealt with cease-fire, establishment of a free and united Korea, and a peaceful settlement of other Far Eastern problems. These were approved by the Committee on 13 January and forwarded to The People's Republic of China along with the question whether the latter would accept these principles as a basis for peaceful settlement.

When that effort had failed to produce any constructive results by the end of January, the United States persuaded the Assembly to adopt a resolution on 1 February 1951 finding

53 Official Records of the Fifth Session ... Resolutions ... p. 9.
54 United Nations Doc. S/1501, 25 June 1950.
55 Official Records of the Fifth Session ... Resolutions ... p. 15.
56 United Nations Doc. A/C.1/651, 13 January 1951.

that the Central People's Government of the People's Republic of China ... has itself engaged in aggression in Korea; [calling] upon the ... People's Republic of China to cause its forces ... in Korea to ... withdraw ... ; [calling] upon all states and authorities to continue to lend every assistance to the United Nations action in Korea; [and requesting] a committee ... to consider additional measures ... to meet this aggression ..., it being understood that the committee is authorized to defer its report if the Good Offices Committee ... reports satisfactory progress in its efforts. ... .[57]

The first "additional measure" which was adopted as a result of this resolution came on 18 May when the Assembly approved the application of an embargo on war materials.[58]

In the Palestine situation the Assembly attempted to deter armed resistance to the partition plan by incorporating in the 29 November 1947 resolution the request to the Security Council that it consider any "attempt to alter by force the settlement" as a threat to the peace. The resolution also authorized the Palestine Commission to direct the establishment of local police forces in both the Arab and Jewish communities to guard the frontiers.[59] However, when armed conflict actually broke out in the spring of 1948 the Assembly, during its second special session, hastily appointed a Mediator "to promote a peaceful adjustment of the future situation of Palestine" under the direction of the Security Council as well as the Assembly.[60] Eventually with the support of two Security Council resolutions urging truces the Mediator was able to halt the hostilities and even persuade the parties to agree to an armistice.

Evaluation

In assessing the Assembly's role in all of these attempts to prevent aggressive intervention one must remember that the plenary organ was not originally designed to deal with matters requiring the collective use of force. Yet because of the

---

[57] United Nations Doc. A/1771, 1 February 1951.
[58] United Nations Doc. A/1807, 21 May 1951.
[59] Official Records of the Second Session ... Resolutions ... p. 131.
[60] Official Records of the Second Special Session ... Resolutions ... p. 5.

inability of the Security Council to take action with respect to Greece and the Communist Chinese intervention in Korea, the only alternatives were either to turn to the Assembly or allow the United Nations to be entirely paralysed by the "veto." A large majority of the Members, led by the United States and the United Kingdom, chose the first alternative rather than the second. In the Palestine situation, while the great powers were never willing to commit themselves to enforce the partition plan, they were willing to have the Security Council take action under Chapter VII to force the establishment of a truce between the Arabs and Jews.

In general one might say that these efforts to halt aggression have produced the most positive results with the least violence in Palestine and Greece, although it is equally apparent that the cessation of hostilities is not a resolution of the tensions which caused the hostilities. While the Assembly cannot claim credit as the primary factor in restoring peace in either case, there is no doubt that it made an important contribution in both. In the Greek situation many reliable witnesses have testified that the watchdog activities of the Special Committee exerted a significant restraining influence upon the aggressors. In the Palestine situation the Assembly mobilized a great segment of world opinion in opposition to the fighting there and provided the agent who, by making excellent use of all of the resources at his command, including the Assembly's influence and the Security Council's directives, was able to arrest the blaze before it turned into an uncontrollable disaster.

The Korean question is the greatest challenge that has yet faced the United Nations and it has called forth the greatest collective military effort ever mobilized in the name of an international organization. The Assembly has not only supported and contributed to the direction of that effort but it has, as a result of the present situation, begun to organize itself so that in accordance with the Uniting for Peace resolution it may begin to fill gaps left by the Security Council.

V. MAJOR DECISIONS ON GENERAL ISSUES

One of the first things that every student learns about the United Nations is that the General Assembly is not a true legislature. What is not frequently mentioned, however, is that the difference is relative rather than absolute. In fact the Assembly looks and acts very much like a legislature, especially when it deals with certain broad general problems that affect its entire membership. And, while its decisions are not legally binding, it may in fact win the compliance of a very large majority of the community it serves—which is more than some national legislatures can boast.

The Assembly's efforts to deal with these broad problems have encompassed roughly three types of questions: the regulation of armaments, the formulation of general principles of political cooperation, and the development of international law.

Regulation of Armaments

In the troubled sphere of armaments regulation, the Assembly concentrated first on the control of atomic energy. In January 1946 the "Big Five" and Canada introduced in the Assembly a "package" resolution providing for the establishment of an Atomic Energy Commission responsible to the Security Council and outlining its terms of reference.[1] Grateful for such influential agreement on this crucial issue, the Assembly was quite content not to tamper with the package and the proposal was accepted unanimously. When the Atomic Energy Commission had completed its technical work and outlined a program of control, it found itself completely unable to secure agreement on the political level in the Security Council. In the autumn of 1948, therefore, the

---

[1] Resolutions Adopted by the General Assembly During the First Part of Its First Session from 10 January to 14 February 1946, p. 9.

reports of the Commission were forwarded to the Assembly through the Security Council "as a matter of special concern."[2] The Commission asserted that, until the political deadlock could be broken, its work should be suspended. The Assembly, however, insisted that the Commission renew its efforts to establish an effective system of control and endorsed by a substantial majority,

the general findings ... and recommendations ... of the first report [of the Atomic Energy Commission] and the specific proposals of part II of the second report ... as constituting the necessary basis for establishing an effective system of international control of atomic energy. ...[3]

It also called upon the six permanent members of the Commission—the permanent members of the Security Council and Canada—to consult together for the purpose of finding some basis for agreement. In 1949 it again stressed the importance of reaching agreement upon a matter which was vital to all the peoples of the United Nations.

Parallel to its efforts in the specific field of atomic energy the Assembly has also tried to formulate plans for the regulation of all armaments.

At the end of 1946, in the second part of the first session, the Soviet Union made its sensational demands for general disarmament and an arms census. The end result was a compromise that attempted to please everyone. The Assembly recognized "the necessity of an early general regulation and reduction of armaments and armed forces," and recommended that the Security Council "give prompt consideration to formulating ... practical measures." At the same time, pointing out the close relationship between disarmaments and security, it recommended that the Security Council "accelerate ... the placing at its disposal of the armed forces mentioned in Article 43 of the Charter."[4] Members

---

2 United Nations Doc. AEC/31, 25 May 1948, Part I, p. 8.

3 Official Records of the Third Session of the General Assembly, Part I, 21 September-12 December 1948, Resolutions, p. 16.

4 Resolutions Adopted by the General Assembly During the Second Part of Its First Session from 23 October to 15 December 1946, pp. 65, 66.

of the United Nations were also urged to withdraw their troops as soon as practicable from ex-enemy territories and from the territories of Members who had not freely consented to such occupation. In a separate resolution the Assembly called upon the Security Council to "determine... the information which the States Members should be called upon to furnish" to facilitate arms regulation.[5]

In response to these resolutions the Security Council created in February 1947 the Commission on Conventional Armaments.

During the third session, in reply to a startling Soviet Union proposal for a one-third reduction of the armaments and armed forces of the five permanent members of the Security Council, the Assembly reminded the world that such a reduction "can only be attained in an atmosphere of real and lasting improvement in international relations" and called upon the Commission for Conventional Armaments to continue studying the problem.[6] Resolutions in 1949 and 1950 reaffirmed the earlier decisions and urged continued efforts to seek a basis for universal agreement. The 1950 resolution also created a special committee to study the advisability of merging the Atomic Energy Commission and the Commission for Conventional Armaments which have, to all intents and purposes, been marking time.

This latest proposal of the Assembly removes one of the obstacles which has heretofore blocked agreement. Since the beginning the Soviet Union has insisted that there can be no piecemeal consideration of the armaments problem. The Western nations, however, have maintained that atomic energy is *sui generis.* Nevertheless, before there can be any substantial progress, several fundamental issues remain to be solved, stemming out of mutual distrust. The West stresses the establishment of a veto-less system of international control, including direct operation and management of dangerous facilities, before the present manufacture of atomic

---

[5] *Ibid.,* p. 67.
[6] Official Records of the Third Session... Part I... Resolutions, p. 18.

weapons is halted and existing stocks destroyed. The Soviet bloc wants the control system to be subject to an eventual, though not "day-to-day," veto; opposes direct operation and management; and insists that existing production and stockpiling cease simultaneously with the establishment of such a control system.

The peculiar contribution of the Assembly has been to educate and to win support for international control from a far larger circle of nations than is represented in the Security Council, to give general direction to the Council's efforts, and to act as a kind of court of appeal for both sides in the debate. While the pressure exerted by the Assembly has not yet produced sufficient agreement to assure an effective control system, it has facilitated agreement among at least forty United Nations Members and it has kept the great powers talking when at times some of them were prepared to discontinue the negotiations altogether.

PRINCIPLES OF POLITICAL COOPERATION

Closely related to the armaments question have been the various "peace" plans that have been proposed in the Assembly appealing to all United Nations Members, especially the great powers, to cooperate in muzzling the dogs of war. The Soviet Union has been particularly active in urging the Assembly to adopt resolutions condemning preparations for war and calling for action for peace. In 1947 the Soviet Union proposed "measures to be taken against propaganda and the inciters of a new war"; in 1949 it proposed condemnation of the preparations for a new war and the conclusion of a five-year pact for peace; and in 1950 it proposed a declaration of the removal of the threats of a new war and strengthening of peace and security among nations. In general the Assembly has dissected these proposals most conscientiously and examined in detail all of the major issues that have influenced international relations in recent decades. On each occasion the Assembly has modified the Soviet proposals, which were invariably directed against the

Western powers, and adopted instead more general recommendations.[7] By 1950 delegations were exhibiting noticeably less patience than previously with these proposals since the issues seemed clearer than ever and the hope of persuading either side to compromise, dimmer than ever.

Parallel to these efforts have been two appeals addressed especially to the great powers to reconcile their differences for the sake of world peace. The first was proposed by Mexico during the first part of the third session and the other by Iraq and Syria during the fifth session. Both were adopted unanimously, since everyone is in favor of peace, but neither expressed anything that had not already been agreed to in the letter and spirit of the United Nations Charter.[8] A more specific "Twenty-year Program for achieving Peace through the United Nations" was submitted by the Secretary-General to the Members of the United Nations in June 1950.[9] The major suggestions of his ten-point proposal included:

(1) Periodic meetings of the Security Council attended by foreign ministers or heads or other members of governments, together with further use of United Nations machinery for mediation and conciliation;

(2) A new attempt to establish international control of atomic energy and the arms race in general;

(3) A renewed effort to reach agreement on the armed forces to be made available to the Security Council under Article 43 of the Charter;

(4) Acceptance and application of the principle of universality of United Nations membership;

(5) Promotion of a vigorous technical assistance program.

---

[7] See, respectively, Official Records of the Second Session of the General Assembly, Resolutions, 16 September-29 November 1947, p. 14; Official Records of the Fourth Session of the General Assembly, Resolutions, 20 September-10 December 1949, p. 13; Official Records of the Fifth Session of the General Assembly, Supplement No. 20, Resolutions, 19 September to 15 December 1950, pp. 13, 14.

[8] See, respectively, Official Records of the Third Session . . . Part I . . . Resolutions, p. 15 and Official Records of the Fifth Session . . . Resolutions . . . p. 12.

[9] United Nations Doc. A/1304, 26 July 1950.

This forthright statement is an indication of the important initiating role which the Secretary-General can play in matters of substance as well as administration. Nevertheless the opposition of various influential powers to certain of the suggestions prevented any positive action during the fifth session. The Assembly merely commended the Secretary-General and requested that

the appropriate organs of the United Nations ... give consideration to those portions of the memorandum ... with which they are particularly concerned, [and that] these organs ... inform the General Assembly at its sixth session ... of any progress achieved. ... [10]

The final substantive results of the discussions of these peace plans are frequently less enlightening than the debates themselves since the drafters tend to make their phrases sufficiently elastic to fit the views of almost every state. Furthermore, the general problem of peace is a far more difficult riddle to fathom than are some of the specific component issues. Nevertheless it can be argued that these exchanges have provided opportunities for an unfettered survey of current international problems, occasions that have afforded both forensic and political catharsis. Furthermore, the resolutions of 1949 ("Essentials of Peace") and 1950 ("Peace through Deeds") were expressions of exceptional solidarity on the part of the great majority of United Nations Members.

Under the mandate provided by Articles 11 (1) and 13 (1a) of the Charter to engage in studies regarding the general principles of international cooperation in the political field, the Assembly's Interim Committee, immediately after its establishment at the beginning of 1948, initiated an extensive research program concerning the use of pacific settlement procedures by the United Nations. Out of this study emerged several specific recommendations which were adopted during the second part of the Assembly's third ses-

---

[10] Official Records of the Fifth Session ... Resolutions ... p. 80.

sion in the spring of 1949 and which are discussed elsewhere in this work: the revision of the General Act of 1928, proposed amendments to the Security Council's Rules in order to provide for the appointment of rapporteurs or conciliators on specific questions, and a proposal to establish a panel for inquiry and conciliation. Since then the Interim Committee has continued this research, has published several useful reports and is gradually amassing an important compendium of comparative data although it has not yet embarked on any very extensive public evaluations or recommendations.

DEVELOPMENT OF INTERNATIONAL LAW

With respect to the development of international law the substantive results thus far have been extremely meager since there is absent in international relations today the kind of community consensus that is essential to the development of binding law. "Some sentiment of shared responsibility for the conduct of a common life is a necessary element in any society, and the necessary force behind any system of law; and the strength of any legal system is proportionate to the strength of such a sentiment."[11] In connection with the long-range effort of the International Law Commission to review and make recommendations concerning existing international law, the Assembly has done no more substantively than establish the mandate of the Commission, approve its work program, and review its draft Declaration of the Rights and Duties of States and draft code of offences against the peace and security of mankind, both of which were then forwarded to governments for their comments.

The Assembly has, however, approved at least three general policy formulations that have a direct bearing upon the development of international law in the political field: the Convention on Genocide, prepared by an *ad hoc* committee of the Economic and Social Council; the Universal Declaration of Human Rights, prepared by the Human Rights Com-

---

11 James L. Brierly, *The Law of Nations* (4th ed., Oxford, The Clarendon Press, 1949), p. 43.

mission; and a revision of the General Act of 1928 which takes into account the replacement of the League of Nations and the Permanent Court of International Justice by the United Nations and the International Court of Justice.[12] Even though these formulations of policy have received the Assembly imprimatur, the progress they represent is not very startling. Ratifications of the Conventions have been sparse, and, while the Declaration of Human Rights was adopted by an affirmative vote of forty-eight, with eight abstentions, the effort to give the force of law to those rights in a series of covenants has been the source of prolonged discussion and disagreement. As long as states continue, as Hobbes put it, "because of their independency [to be] in continual jealousies, and in the state and posture of gladiators . . . ,"[13] progress in the development of binding law will be exceedingly slow. Under these circumstances it would be false progress to attempt to force the development beyond what the present political environment will permit. It is perhaps fortunate, however, that nations are frequently willing to accept in practice far greater international obligations than they are willing to accept as formal binding commitments.

---

12 See, respectively, Official Records of the Third Session . . . Part I . . . Resolutions, pp. 174, 71, and Official Records of the Third Session of the General Assembly, Part II, 5 April - 18 May 1949, Resolutions, p. 10.
13 Thomas Hobbes, *Leviathan*, Ch. XIII.

VI. MAJOR DECISIONS ON ORGANIZATIONAL ISSUES

A political organization, like any social institution, is the evidence of decisions past and the matrix of decisions to come. This interaction between the substance of policy decisions and the structure contrived to implement them is nowhere more apparent than in connection with the third major group of the Assembly's decisions in the political sphere touching upon certain organizational issues. These decisions reflect the adjustment of the Assembly's organization to various substantive problems and also reveal the impact of organization upon policy. The following analysis draws upon the Assembly's experience in connection with three major organizational objectives: (1) certain efforts to influence the Security Council; (2) efforts to compensate for the Security Council's paralysis on several issues by strengthening the role of the Assembly in the political field; (3) efforts to strengthen and adapt the Assembly's administrative procedures.

EFFORTS TO INFLUENCE THE SECURITY COUNCIL

Membership

On the question of membership the Assembly began as early as the second part of the first session in the fall of 1946 to call the attention of the Security Council to the provisions of Article 4 of the Charter and to urge the Council to evaluate applications for United Nations membership strictly in accordance with those provisions.[1] Implicit in this recommendation was a warning not to resort to special criteria such as the Soviet Union's policy that it would not support the admission of those states with which it had no

---

[1] Resolutions Adopted by the General Assembly During the Second Part of Its First Session from 23 October to 15 December 1946, p. 61.

diplomatic relations. In adopting this first statement of principle the Assembly chose a middle path between the Argentine view that the Assembly might decide admission questions independently of the Security Council, and the Soviet view that the Assembly should consider no membership questions except those concerning which it had received recommendations from the Security Council. During the same session the Assembly formed a special committee to consult with a similar committee appointed by the Security Council in order to prepare "rules governing the admission of new Members which will be acceptable both to the General Assembly and to the Security Council."[2]

Since that time the Assembly has not only reaffirmed its first statement of principles at each session but it also adopted, during its second session in the fall of 1947, primarily at the insistence of the smaller states, a Belgian proposal to ask the opinion of the International Court of Justice regarding several key points at issue.

The questions asked the Court were:

Is a Member ... entitled to make its consent to the admission [of a state] dependent on conditions not expressly provided by paragraph 1 of ... [Article 4 of the Charter]? In particular, can such a Member ... subject its affirmative vote to the additional condition that other States be admitted to membership in the United Nations together with that State?[3]

On 28 May 1948 the Court decided by the rather close vote of nine to six to answer both questions in the negative.[4] In support of this opinion the majority argued that the criteria listed in Article 4 are complete and exhaustive and thus sufficient to qualify a state for admission, that at the same time Members might take into consideration any factors

---

2 *Ibid.*, p. 62.

3 Official Records of the Second Session of the General Assembly, Resolutions, 16 September - 29 November 1947, p. 19.

4 Admission of a State to the United Nations, Advisory Opinion, ICJ Reports 1948.

that might reasonably be related to the provisions of Article 4, and that each application should be considered separately and on its own merits. A joint dissenting opinion, by Justices Basdevant (France), Winiarski (Poland), McNair (United Kingdom) and Read (Canada), opposed the majority on both questions. On the first, the minority felt that admission is preeminently a "political" act. Thus Members might base their decisions on "political" considerations not specified in Article 4. There is no specific statement in the Charter that the conditions listed in Article 4 are exhaustive nor that states fulfilling those conditions must be admitted to the United Nations. On the second issue, the minority argued that, since the decision is essentially "political," a Member may make its assent dependent on the admission of other states. Justices Zoricic (Yugoslavia) and Krylov (USSR) wrote separate dissenting opinions which followed the general lines of the joint dissent.

The earlier doubts of many Members concerning the wisdom of sending such a matter to the Court were confirmed by these opinions. Neither side made a very positive contribution to the settlement of the problem since the majority as well as the minority left ample room for different interpretations of such vague criteria as "peace-loving" and "able and willing to carry out... obligations" of the Charter. While the Court is still young there are many who feel that it should not be burdened with such highly explosive questions but should be used only for more obviously justiciable issues so that it may have an opportunity to create an atmosphere of goodwill and acceptance.

Again during its fourth session in the fall of 1949 the Assembly turned to the Court for another opinion on the membership question. Since 1946 Argentina had regularly claimed that the Assembly may decide to admit a state independently of any Security Council recommendation on the matter. Although few Members supported this view, it was finally decided to seek a Court opinion that would settle the matter once and for all. The question asked was:

Can the admission of a State ... be effected by a decision of the General Assembly when the Security Council has made no recommendation for admission ... ?[5]

On 3 March 1950, the Court ruled by a vote of twelve to two that admission could not be effected by the Assembly without a Security Council recommendation.[6] At first glance it seems somewhat pointless to have troubled the Court with such a question on which there was relatively little disagreement. At the same time it served the useful purpose of giving an authoritative and disinterested answer to those states like Argentina that had raised the issue so frequently in the past.

Regarding the question of what governments should be recognized by the United Nations as representing states already Members, an issue directly related to the China problem, the Assembly was unable after lengthy debate during the fifth session to agree upon definitive criteria. The United Kingdom and various other members espoused the view that *de facto* control of an area, supported by the obedience of the bulk of the population, should be the determining criterion. On the other hand the United States, China and certain other countries believed that the democratic character of the government should also be taken into account. All the Assembly was finally able to agree upon was a relatively weak resolution, adopted by an unenthusiastic majority of 36 to 6 with 9 abstentions, which declared that

the attitude adopted by the General Assembly or its Interim Committee concerning any such question should be taken into account in other organs of the United Nations and in the specialized agencies; ... [that the question] should be considered in the light of the Purposes and Principles of the Charter and the circumstances of each case; ... [and] the attitude adopted by the General Assembly or its Interim Committee concerning any such question shall not of itself affect the direct relations of individual Member States with the State concerned. ...[7]

---

[5] Official Records of the Fourth Session of the General Assembly, Resolutions, 20 September - 10 December 1949, p. 21.

[6] United Nations Doc. A/1353, 9 September 1950.

[7] Official Records of the Fifth Session of the General Assembly, Supplement No. 20, Resolutions, 19 September to 15 December 1950, p. 25.

Voting

On the question of voting in the Security Council, the smaller nations took the lead during the second part of the first session in persuading the Assembly to adopt a resolution that recommended to the Council "the early adoption of practices and procedures . . . to assist in reducing the difficulties in the application of Article 27 and to ensure the prompt and effective exercise by the Security Council of its functions. . . ."[8] Then, on the basis of the study on the voting problem made during 1948 by the Interim Committee at the Assembly's request, the Assembly adopted, during the second part of its third session, a resolution that suggested thirty-five kinds of decisions which the Council should consider "procedural" and thus not subject to the unanimity rule. It also appealed to the permanent members of the Council to take special steps to solve the voting problem and also recommended to Members of the United Nations that in agreements conferring functions on the Council they provide conditions of voting which would exclude the application of the unanimity rule.[9] While the five permanent members followed the Assembly's suggestions to the extent of arranging for consultation among themselves when important votes are to be taken, they have not yet reached an agreement regarding the thirty-five items that the Assembly proposed should be treated as "procedural."

Appraisal

One cannot dismiss the Assembly's efforts on membership and voting merely because they have failed to budge the Council from its position on these issues. The Assembly's debates have not only made the world aware of the importance of these questions but have also made unmistakably clear the views of the great majority of the Members. While it must be remembered that neither the United States nor the Soviet Union would have joined the United Nations

8 Resolutions . . . Second Part . . . First Session . . . p. 64.
9 Official Records of the Third Session of the General Assembly, Part II, 5 April - 18 May 1949, Resolutions, p. 7.

without the "veto" as their shield, there is at the same time no reason to prevent free discussion in the Assembly of the problems of which the "veto" is but a symptom. The question of membership is, of course, becoming increasingly serious as such nations as Italy, Japan, Germany, Austria and others gather at the gate to be admitted. The over-all problem of the "veto" is the organizational manifestation of the fundamental lack of mutual trust among nations. Gradually the Assembly has lost hope of reforming the Security Council directly and has turned to exploring various means, especially those to be discussed in the following section, of strengthening the Assembly's own authority in the political field.

Efforts to Strengthen the Assembly

Interim Committee

The Assembly's resolution creating the Interim Committee during the second session was the first major attempt to reinforce the plenary body's organizational structure with respect to the political field. This move was made to compensate for the Security Council's failure to take action on several critical issues, particularly in connection with the Soviet "veto" in August 1947 of the United States draft resolution to create a commission to assist in restoring peace on the borders of Greece. Thus it was the United States that suggested the plan to establish an interim body that could perform certain limited functions in behalf of the Assembly in the political field between sessions,[10] a proposal not unlike an earlier one made by the Netherlands in December 1945, during the Conference of the Preparatory Commission of the United Nations.

The strongest opposition to the United States project was voiced by the Soviet Union and its close allies who argued that: (1) it would interfere with the Security Council's primary responsibility for the maintenance of peace and

---

10 Official Records of the Second Session of the General Assembly, Plenary Meetings, Verbatim Record, 16 September-19 November 1947, pp. 19-27.

security; (2) Article 22 of the Charter authorized no such powerful organ as a "subsidiary body"; (3) it would give the Assembly more extensive investigatory authority than that possessed by the Security Council under Article 34; (4) it was an outright attack upon the unanimity rule; and (5) only the Security Council should exercise continuous authority in the field of peace and security. While most of the other countries were inclined to be cautious in thus reinforcing the Assembly's political role, they agreed in general with the reply of the United States that: (1) the proposed committee would supplement but not supplant the Security Council's primary position in the political sphere; (2) Article 22 authorized any subsidiary body which the Assembly believed to be appropriate and necessary; (3) the new committee would give the Assembly no powers which it did not already possess; (4) it was a means of avoiding a direct effort to alter the unanimity rule; and (5) the continuity of the Assembly's responsibilities in the political field was in no way limited by the Charter although Article 20, which called for "regular annual sessions," precluded the Assembly's remaining in continuous session.

It is obvious, as one considers the discussion which surrounded the birth of the Interim Committee, that the principal motivation behind its creation was the concern, particularly on the part of the United States, about the Security Council's stalemate on the Balkan problem and a desire to gird the Assembly so that it, rather than the Council, might do battle in such situations, between as well as during its sessions. Yet in the years since its establishment the Committee has never on its own initiative considered any situation or dispute or created a commission of inquiry. The basic reasons for this inactivity are, first, that the participating members have advanced cautiously with the hope of winning the confidence of the non-participating Soviet group and, second, that many states feel that decisions on most current problems would lack political relevance unless they were made in collaboration with the Soviet Union.

There has also been a feeling that the Interim Committee's personnel has not always been of as high a quality as that to be found in a regular session of the Assembly, and that the results of its efforts thus far have not been commensurate with the time and energy expended. Yet the pressure of events now makes it more necessary than ever that the Assembly be able to exert its influence in the political field on a continuous rather than a periodic basis. To accomplish this objective without resorting to the Interim Committee, the Assembly decided in December 1950 to extend its session in order to allow its First Committee to remain active in connection with the Korean situation after the other standing committees had completed their work and disbanded. This device has the obvious advantages of making possible the participation of the Soviet group, encouraging the same personnel that served on the Committee during the early part of the session to continue serving, and allowing full exercise of all the authority of the Assembly unlimited by the restrictions which apply to the Interim Committee.

This development is particularly interesting in view of the previous reaction in 1947 to a Bolivian proposal that the Assembly divide each session into two parts, the first to be occupied with the regular program, the second to serve merely as authority for the continuation of the First Committee until the beginning of the next session. Most of the other delegations opposed this plan, however, and cited as their authority the spirit as well as the letter of Article 20 of the Charter to the effect that the Assembly "shall meet in regular annual sessions." Technically, to satisfy this requirement the Assembly need do no more than adjourn each session a few days before the next regular session is scheduled to begin.

Uniting for Peace Resolution

The second major declaration of the Assembly that considerably strengthened its muscles in the political field was the Uniting for Peace resolution adopted by a vote of 52 to 5, with India and Argentina abstaining, on 3 November 1950.[11] The most immediate stimulus leading to this proposal was the North Korean attack upon the Republic of Korea on 25 June 1950 when many Members, including the United States, anticipated that it might be necessary to take action under the auspices of the General Assembly should the Soviet Union decide to vote against action by the Security Council. Although that possibility did not materialize at the time, due to the absence of the Soviet representative in connecton with the dispute over the representation of the People's Republic of China, the United States decided to avoid any future stalemate under similar circumstances by proposing its Uniting for Peace resolution to the fifth session of the Assembly.[12] Other states that joined with the United States as co-sponsors were Canada, France, Philippines, Turkey, United Kingdom and Uruguay.

The Soviet Union voiced the strongest, although not absolute, opposition to the proposal. Besides arguing that the plan would interfere with the Security Council's primary role in the political sphere, the Soviet delegation also cited the terms of Article 11 (2) of the Charter providing that "any . . . question on which action is necessary shall be referred to the Security Council by the General Assembly either before or after discussion." While many of the other delegations, particularly Sweden, South Africa and Pakistan, indicated that they were seriously concerned about the implications of that passage of the Charter, most of them did not consider it an insuperable obstacle. The Canadians argued that the word "action" as used in Article 11 (2) implied only action which the Security Council was intended to take under Chapter VII of the Charter. The Philippines representative believed that the Assembly's past action in connection with Palestine, Korea and Greece had rendered

---

11 Official Records of the Fifth Session of the General Assembly, Plenary Meetings, Verbatim Record, p. 347.

12 United Nations Docs. A/C.1/576, 7 October 1950 and A/C.1/576/Rev.1, 14 October 1950.

the passage meaningless. Pakistan stated that although the Assembly could not *take* action, it might *recommend* action. The United Kingdom representative pointed out that the Assembly was obligated merely to *refer* such a question to the Security Council after which, should the Security Council fail to solve the problem, the Assembly might resume jurisdiction of the matter and recommend action.

Because these questions of constitutional interpretation are surface manifestations of deeper fundamental political attitudes with respect to the United Nations it is interesting to recall the thinking behind Article 11 (2) at Dumbarton Oaks and San Francisco which was mentioned briefly in Chapter I. It seems to have been generally understood at the time that the only kind of collective action which would ever be effective would be action that was agreed to and supported unanimously by the great powers. Such action was to be taken through the Security Council because only in that organ were the great powers to be protected by the "veto." Since the possibility of mobilizing collective force by means of a mere recommendation, rather than a binding decision, seemed neither desirable nor practical, it was not seriously discussed.

At the same time it was clearly understood at San Francisco that the Assembly had authority to discuss and make recommendations, though not binding decisions, "on any questions or any matters within the scope of the present Charter," according to the language of Article 10. The fact that it was decided not to give the Assembly specific authority to make recommendations regarding the use of force is not a decisive consideration. Many specific powers were not mentioned explicitly in the Charter on the ground that they were implied in other broader grants of authority. And no authority could be broader than Article 10. Nor was the Assembly explicitly prohibited from making recommendations regarding the use of force.

It seems clear therefore that Article 11 (2) was understood to mean that "action" of the type that was to be taken by a binding decision, not a mere recommendation, under Chapter VII was to be referred to the Security Council. This did not however prevent the Assembly from making *recommendations* regarding the use of force, subject to Article 12, undesirable as such a course of action may have seemed at the time.

Although one can thus argue that the Uniting for Peace resolution is constitutionally valid, it is at the same time clear that such an innovation is a significant modification of the spirit, if not the letter, of the Charter which obviously intended that the Security Council should direct the use of collective force under the United Nations.

The effect of the first specific provision of the Uniting for Peace resolution was to commit the Assembly in advance, whenever the "Security Council, because of a lack of unanimity of the permanent members, fails to exercise its primary responsibility for the maintenance of international peace," to "consider the matter immediately with a view to making appropriate recommendations..., including...the use of armed force...." While the Charter states that the Assembly "may" discuss, consider or recommend, the Uniting for Peace resolution categorically provides that it "shall" consider "immediately."[13]

These provisions will, of course, require considerable interpretation in each specific instance to determine whether or not the Security Council has actually failed to exercise its responsibilities properly. Heretofore it has been tacitly assumed that this decision rested with the Security Council which could, if it wished to, clear the path for the Assembly by removing the item in question from its agenda. It has also been assumed that the Council's decision to keep an item on its agenda is conclusive evidence that it is "exercising in respect of any dispute or situation the functions assigned to it in the...Charter."[14] The Uniting for Peace resolution does not state how the decision is to be made. It

---

[13] Official Records of the Fifth Session...Resolutions...p. 10.
[14] Article 12 (1).

may be presumed that the customary procedure will continue to be followed, but it has been suggested in some quarters that there is nothing to prevent the Assembly itself from deciding that the Security Council has failed to exercise the functions assigned to it even though the disputed item may remain on its agenda. This is a somewhat academic question at present, however, since a matter may be removed from the Council's agenda by a simple procedural majority of any seven members.

India, Norway, South Africa, Israel and other delegations urged that the Security Council be allowed as much time as possible to exhaust its resources regarding a particular situation before resorting to the Assembly. In reply the sponsors of the resolution made it clear that this was their intention. On the other hand some members, especially China and Ecuador, pointed out that the possibilities of obstructionism in the Security Council, which had been demonstrated the previous August in connection with Korea, might make it desirable for the Assembly to act before the Council had actually voted on a question or even placed it on its agenda.

As to the possible recommendation of the use of armed force, Yugoslavia argued that such measures should be considered only in connection with an act of aggression. Israel urged a mandate that would also apply to breaches of the peace, but not mere threats to the peace as originally proposed by the United States. It was this latter view that was finally accepted.

In assuming responsibilities of this nature, the Assembly has to be able to act swiftly and to exercise more or less continuous supervision. This involves some rather basic organizational changes for a body which had been envisaged primarily as meeting once a year for broad, over-all policy discussions. The resolution, therefore, provides that

If not in session at the time, the General Assembly may meet in emergency special session within twenty-four hours of the request therefor. Such emergency special session shall be called if requested by the Security Council on the vote of any seven members, or by a majority of the Members of the United Nations.[15]

Under the old Rules of Procedure of the Assembly, special sessions were to be held "within fifteen days of the receipt by the Secretary-General of a request . . . "[16] and the provisional agenda was to be communicated to members from ten to fifteen days in advance depending on the convoking agency.[17] Article 20 of the Charter provides that such convocation may be made by a majority of Members or "at the request of the Security Council" but, in the latter case, there is no indication whether this decision is to be considered as procedural or substantive and thus subject to the veto.

The Soviet Union and Syria argued that such a decision by the Security Council would require unanimity on the part of the permanent members, while most of the other delegates agreed with the United States that a majority of any seven should be sufficient. Nevertheless there can be no doubt that Syria was right in suggesting that the use of the word "shall" in the resolution did not take into account the Security Council's acknowledged right to determine its own Rules within the framework of the Charter. The Soviet Union also asked for a two-week rather than a twenty-four hour interval, but the majority disagreed. This twenty-four hour provision now makes the Assembly for all practical purposes as continuous as the Security Council, even without the Interim Committee, a significant modification of the views held at San Francisco.

The full Assembly, however, is inherently too cumbersome a body to assume continuous supervision over field investigations. As a partial solution the Assembly created the fourteen-member Peace Observation Commission. The original plan of the United States was to exclude the great powers in the interests of greater tranquillity and objectivity. Nevertheless, when the Soviet Union indicated that it wanted to

---

[15] Official Records of the Fifth Session . . . Resolutions . . . p. 10.
[16] Rules of Procedure of the General Assembly, 1 January 1950, Rule 8, p. 2.
[17] *Ibid.*, Rule 16, p. 4.

join rather than denounce the body, most of the other delegations were only too eager to include all of the great powers. Also represented on the Commission for the calendar years 1951 and 1952 are states drawn from the following areas: Latin America (Colombia and Uruguay), Middle East (Iraq and Israel), Scandinavia (Sweden), Asia (India and Pakistan), Pacific (New Zealand), and the Soviet sphere (Czechoslovakia).

The Commission may be utilized by the General Assembly, or the Interim Committee between sessions, "if the Security Council is not exercising the functions assigned to it by the Charter with respect to the matter in question," or by the Security Council. The Assembly rejected a Swedish proposal that the Secretary-General be given the power to direct the Commission as too controversial a responsibility to burden him with. It also was unreceptive to a Soviet and Israeli drive to exclude the Interim Committee from among those authorized to utilize the Commission. The United States insisted that this provision was necessary in order to provide supervision for the Commission's work between sessions of the Assembly.

As another approach to the problem of equipping the Assembly for its new role, the resolution set up a Collective Measures Committee to study and report on the methods "which might be used to maintain and strengthen international peace and security." Because of the resistance on the part of Australia and others to any United Nations investigation of national strategic resources, it was decided to limit the functions of the Collective Measures Committee as specified above and not to authorize it to study and report on "resources, including armed forces, which are or might be made available to the United Nations" as had been provided in the original draft. The Australian delegation expressed the cautious attitude of some countries when it declared that states would be reluctant to report the status of their military resources and any effort of the United Nations to try to plan future military action would be "playing with fire."

The report of the Committee is to be made to the Security Council as well as the Assembly not later than 1 September 1951. As for its membership, it was decided not to include any of the Soviet bloc which indicated no desire to participate in this body. The members selected were: Australia, Belgium, Brazil, Burma, Canada, Egypt, France, Mexico, Philippines, Turkey, the United Kingdom, the United States, Venezuela and Yugoslavia.

While there was some discussion of the possible organization of a United Nations military force along lines similar to those suggested from time to time by groups such as the Commission to Study the Organization of Peace, there was no significant support for the idea largely because of the complexity and cost that were felt to be involved in such a plan. Sweden and a few Latin American delegations called attention to certain constitutional provisions in some countries that would limit their freedom to make armed forces available to the United Nations. Thus an amendment was added to the effect that such contingents would be provided by a state "in accordance with its constitutional processes."[18]

Sweden and India raised the practical question of how much could actually be accomplished through the awkward collaboration of individual national contingents. The only effort in the resolution to meet this objection was the request to the Secretary-General to appoint "a panel of military experts who could be made available, on request, to Member States wishing to obtain technical advice regarding the organization, training, and equipment" for the United Nations units. There can be no doubt, however, that this whole problem, which has just begun to be explored, will present numerous and troublesome difficulties. But one must also ask: is there any better alternative within the present political environment?

The element of voluntarism is not necessarily a fatal weakness. Although the contributions made by the Members in connection with the Korean conflict were not initially re-

---

[18] Official Records of the Fifth Session ... Resolutions ... p. 11.

markable in quantity, they were remarkable as the first
instance of such military action, under the United Nations
—or the League of Nations for that matter—in spite of the
failure to implement Article 43. With careful advance planning and organization and cautious judgment in committing
the Assembly to such action, the United Nations may be able
to mobilize considerable military strength entirely on a
"volunteer" basis.

There is, however, a basic problem which remains to be
solved. The Assembly has been weak in providing continuous supervision regarding certain situations with which it
has been concerned. This shortcoming was particularly evident during the autumn and winter of 1950-51 in the Korean
situation when neither the Assembly nor the Security Council was giving close direction to the forces in the field. The
complex and crucial military-political decisions which needed
to be made frequently fell by default to the United Nations
Commander. In the Palestine situation, on the other hand,
the Assembly and especially the Security Council gave much
closer and more regular support and direction to their agents
in the field.

While there are a number of basic problems such as this
to be solved, the most important issue is: is such an innovation politically desirable? To answer that, one must consider
the alternatives. If the Security Council fails to take effective
action in a situation such as Korea, the possible alternatives
are either to do nothing further through the United Nations,
thus leaving the matter to be dealt with outside the collective
organization, or to try to carry out the will of the preponderant majority of Members through the General Assembly.
Since the great majority, in spite of what has been said in
some quarters about United States pressure, actually seems
to have been in favor of the latter alternative, this would
appear to be the better course of action.

No one doubts, however, that this path is full of political
land mines. First, there may be a temptation on the part of
the Assembly to act precipitately before the Security Council

has had an opportunity to exhaust its possibilities. Second, as in the case of Korea, there is a danger of dual jurisdiction with possibly conflicting instructions or a policy vacuum with no instructions. Third, Assembly recommendations may be made by a numerically large but politically irresponsible majority. Fourth, once recommendations are made they may fail to be implemented effectively. Fifth, the current emphasis on the use of force may divert attention from more positive long-range programs of conciliation and economic and social development. Sixth, there is the immediate danger of over-selling this plan to the public as an easy and simple panacea, which it obviously is not. Nevertheless, if we believe that as a last resort barefaced aggression must be met with force, then the Uniting for Peace resolution seems to be a reasonable, though far from perfect, method for compensating for occasional impasses in the Security Council.

Efforts to Improve Administrative Procedures

As the Assembly's load has steadily increased there have been more and more intensive drives to heighten the efficiency of administrative procedures and to minimize unnecessary waste and friction. In the spring of 1949 the Assembly set up a special committee on "Methods and Procedures of the General Assembly" which brought in a number of specific recommendations which were adopted on such matters as submission of new items, assignment of items to committees, role of chairmen, handling of debates and voting.

In order to expedite the staffing of commissions and improve the quality of the membership, in the spring of 1949 the Assembly invited

each Member State to designate from one to five persons who, by reason of their training, experience, character and standing, are deemed to be well fitted to serve as members of commissions of inquiry or of conciliation and who would be disposed to serve in that capacity;[19]

---

19 Official Records of the Third Session ... Part II ... Resolutions, p. 13.

At its next session the Assembly authorized the Secretary-General to establish a similar panel of "persons qualified to assist United Nations missions in the functions of observation and supervision."[20]

The potential advantages of such a device are that it makes available persons who are especially qualified for such duties; it provides personnel representative of *all* the Members rather than only those few larger states that find it easiest to spare such individuals; and the nominations are an implicit promise that the cooperating countries will actually supply such persons when called upon to do so. The difficulties involved in such a plan are to get a list that will serve for many different kinds of political situations and also to keep such a list current.

Although the effort to create what would have been in essence a United Nations police force of from 1,000 to 5,000 men failed largely because of opposition from the Soviet bloc, a United Nations Field Service with limited functions has been established to facilitate United Nations operations in the field. The Secretary-General was authorized to enlist in the Service not more than 300 persons to perform miscellaneous communications, security and clerical functions.

Evaluation

The significance of these organizational decisions is that they are structural reflections of the Assembly's increasing determination during the past five years to fill the vacuum left by the Security Council in certain kinds of situations. Not only are they the result of a policy trend but they have also helped to shape policy as in the case of the Interim Committee's role regarding the decision to hold elections in only one part of Korea. The thread that runs through all of these organizational decisions is the Assembly's quest for greater continuity, stronger action to promote compliance and more effective subordinate agencies. The Assembly's

---

[20] Official Records of the Fourth Session ... Resolutions ... p. 22.

efforts to adjust to the difficult situations which have confronted it have inevitably been somewhat impromptu and fumbling. Yet it has never refused a challenge nor taken refuge in inaction.

In meeting these tests there is no convincing evidence that the Assembly has introduced innovations which are specifically prohibited by the Charter. Yet it is obvious that changes have taken place which have gone beyond the expectations and the intentions of the Charter's framers. Every constitution ever written however has had to be "amended by interpretation" under the pressure of events. Constitutions that do not bend are very apt to break. As long as the overwhelming majority of the community favors such a change by interpretation and as long as that change does not inflict undue violence upon the language of the constitution, the change would seem not only feasible but desirable. When an institution ceases to respond to the will of the great majority, it has lost its vitality as a democratic instrument.

VII.   CONCLUSIONS

In the fall of 1946 Warren Austin argued in the Assembly against certain efforts that were being made to modify the application of the veto in the Security Council by saying,

The principle of unanimity of the great Powers has from the first ... been limited in its application as a voting procedure to matters essential to the maintenance of international peace and security. . . . There is no requirement for unanimity in the Assembly, in the Economic and Social Council and in the Trusteeship Council. . . . These organs ... do not have the power to enforce. . . . It was held [at San Francisco moreover] that since the Council cannot take enforcement action without the concurrence of all the permanent members it might endanger the effectiveness of the Council's work if decisions under Chapter VI that might lead to ... enforcement action under Chapter VII were taken by a vote which found the permanent members divided.[1]

By 1950 the emphasis was quite different when Secretary of State Dean Acheson spoke to the Assembly's fifth session:

. . . if the Security Council is not able to act ... the Charter does not leave the United Nations impotent. . . . The Charter ... also vests in the General Assembly authority and responsibility for matters affecting international peace. The General Assembly can and should organize itself to discharge its responsibility promptly and decisively if the Security Council is prevented from acting.[2]

The difference between these two statements is a striking measure of the distance that the General Assembly has traveled since 1945.

Major Influences on the Assembly

In order to make history a servant rather than a master, it is important to understand the basic forces that have given

---

[1] Official Records of the Second Part of the First Session of the General Assembly, Plenary Meetings, Verbatim Record, 23 October - 16 December 1946, pp. 904-06.

[2] Official Records of the Fifth Session of the General Assembly, Plenary Meetings, Verbatim Record, p. 24.

rise to the evolution which has been traced. Certainly an objective appraisal of the facts reveals that it is the great powers which have led the way. It is also important to emphasize, because this aspect is so frequently neglected in writings on this subject, that the Soviet Union has been just as active as the Western powers in promoting the development of the Assembly's political role. While it is true that the United States and the United Kingdom were primarily responsible for referring to the Assembly such problems as those regarding Korea, Greece and Palestine, it was the Soviet Union which urged the Assembly to take extraordinarily strong measures regarding Spain, the Soviet complaint of United States aggression against China, the status of the former Italian Colonies, Palestine and other similar questions.

Why have the great powers resorted to this strategy? Their primary motivation has been to overcome certain, though not all, of the stalemates which have occurred in the Security Council. Although they realized the dangers involved in adopting resolutions in the Assembly which did not have the unanimous support of all the great powers, they preferred nevertheless to take that course rather than allow the United Nations to be blocked entirely by the Council's inability to act. Moreover they turned to the plenary body not only because they wanted to escape the "veto," but also because they found the Assembly a useful channel for winning and maintaining the collaboration of the middle and small powers that are not all regularly represented in the Security Council. One has only to think of the smaller countries that have actively supported the United Nations efforts in Korea in order to appreciate how important it is for these nations to be included in the decision-making process regarding many political questions on a regular and continuous basis. The great powers have also realized that the Assembly debates are a powerful psychological force throughout the world, often reported more completely than those of the Council since most of the Members have their "favorite sons" in the plenary body. Finally each side, knowing that the other will undoubtedly make good use of the Assembly platform, feels that it cannot afford to sulk in the wings.

The second most important force behind this development has been the desire of the smaller powers to strengthen the plenary organ as the instrument best suited to their own particular interests since they are numerically preponderant in that body and wield far more influence there than in the Security Council. Many of the smaller states have been fundamentally opposed from the very beginning to the whole concept that underlies the Security Council and its "veto" even though they reluctantly accepted those provisions at San Francisco when they were told that the great powers insisted upon them. Herbert V. Evatt has said, "I doubt whether any of the middle or small powers represented at San Francisco really believed in the justice of the Great Power veto, though some of them voted for it on grounds of political expediency."[3]

In keeping with these views many of the smaller states feel that the Assembly is the highest source of authority in the United Nations because it is the only organ in which all Members are represented. Thus the Rapporteur of Commission II at San Francisco stated,

The majority of the Powers . . . emphasized in the first place that the Council acts only on behalf of the Assembly; unquestionably, all the powers of the International Organization reside originally in the Assembly and for that reason, the Security Council must be relied upon to express, in the final analysis, . . . only the tendencies of the Assembly.[4]

Although this statement tends to inflate the constitutional authority of the Assembly beyond reasonable limits, it is significant as a point of view that is widely held among the smaller countries. It should be noted, however, that it does not imply a willingness to give the Assembly the power to bind them by its decisions and, in fact, some of them have

---

[3] *The United Nations* (Cambridge, Harvard University Press, 1948), p. 23.
[4] UNCIO, Documents, XII, p. 446.

strongly opposed its recommendations on particular issues as in connection with Spain.

A third major factor which has drawn the Assembly ever nearer to the center of the stage has been the present disturbed state of the world. The fact that so many serious tensions have arisen so soon after World War II has made it almost inevitable that the Assembly should be called upon to shoulder far heavier burdens than were originally anticipated. We have also seen that the more peaceful period in which the League of Nations was born was a factor in shielding that body from the problems which have plagued its successor.

Most commentators, however, have tended to look upon the General Assembly's experience as a wholly temporary and anomalous aberration due primarily to the current emergency. Yet the same forces were at work in the League of Nations and at the United Nations Conference in San Francisco, though far less actively than now. The interests of the great, middle and small powers are likely in any era to produce this same tendency to move from the narrower to the broader organ as the central political forum. And extraordinary crises, such as the one we are presently enduring, merely accentuate this tendency.

EVALUATION OF ACHIEVEMENTS

Looking back along the road that the Assembly has traveled since 1945 it is important to assess that body's actual accomplishments without undue optimism or pessimism. We have already seen that perhaps the most notable progress has been achieved in helping to create new political orders in Palestine, Korea, the former Italian Colonies, as well as in promoting the development of the trust territories and other non-self-governing areas. The Assembly has been assisted in these efforts by a growing sense of international community responsibility among nations with respect to dependent peoples. It has been possible not only to arrive at acceptable compromise solutions for extremely difficult problems, but also to take vigorous measures to implement these recommendations.

No appraisal of these activities would be complete, however, without citing a few of the major obstacles that stand in the way. Although the sense of international community responsibility may be growing, it is still impeded by intense opposition in some quarters. Perhaps the most dramatic example of this resistance is the attitude that South Africa has adopted regarding the disposition of South West Africa. And when a great power expresses opposition, as in the case of Korea, the situation becomes very difficult indeed. The experience of the past five years demonstrates, however, what remarkable things can be done on the basis of the modest "recommendation."

Since the Assembly was never designed to take an active part in directing collective military forces, it is perhaps not surprising that it has been less effective in resisting aggressive intervention than in creating new political regimes. While there can be little doubt that the "northern neighbors of Greece . . . [were] restrained by the presence of the [United Nations Special] Committee and its power of exposure," as John Foster Dulles once put it,[5] it is also clear that the primary reasons for the cessation of hostilities were the aid given by the United States and the Yugoslav defection from the Soviet camp. In the case of Palestine the extent of the Assembly's enforcement activities was to call upon the Security Council for support and to create the Mediator who was able to harness that support to his own negotiations. In the Korean situation the Assembly has left primary responsibility in the hands of the Unified Command, established at the behest of the Security Council, but it has also issued its own recommendations to the forces in Korea regarding such important matters as the crossing of the thirty-eighth parallel. In all of these situations the most obvious limitation has been the Assembly's lack of strong authority

---

[5] Department of State *Bulletin,* Vol. XIX, No. 489 (14 November 1948), p. 609.

and resources. Yet that body has displayed considerable ingenuity in making the most of the powers it does possess, even to the extent of attempting to mobilize and direct armed contingents by means of its general authority to issue recommendations.

In trying to promote the observance of international obligations regarding fundamental freedoms, the Assembly has been disappointingly unsuccessful. Its ambitious 1946 resolution declaring the diplomatic ostracism of Spain proved so ineffective that the non-interventionist group was able by 1950 to persuade the Assembly to retreat substantially from that original position. Concerning the treatment of Indians in South Africa the Assembly's actions seem to have increased rather than reduced the political temperature. Finally, having failed to produce any positive results regarding the alleged violation of human rights in Bulgaria, Hungary and Rumania, the Assembly has had to content itself with being little more than a bulletin board for evidence that may be submitted to it. In spite of these setbacks, however, the Assembly has exposed to the world certain threatening situations with which the international community should concern itself.

Despite the initial agreement to set up the Atomic Energy Commission, the Assembly has been no more successful than the Security Council in its efforts to develop an effective program for the regulation of armaments. Although it succeeded in November 1948 in endorsing the proposed atomic energy control plan recommended by a majority of the members of the United Nations Atomic Energy Commission, it has not been able to stimulate any appreciable progress since that time. Nor have the Assembly's perennial "peace" resolutions brought us any nearer to peace, although they have provided opportunities for far-ranging reviews of current international problems. As for the development of international law, this is necessarily a slow process that must travel nearer the end than the beginning of the parade of civilization.

The Assembly's decisions on organizational issues related to the political field have been nothing more than institutional reflections of the forces which have been discussed above. The efforts to modify the Security Council's practices with regard to the veto, especially on the question of admission to membership, have of course borne little fruit except to call the world's attention to the tensions that exist among the great powers. The establishment of the Interim Committee has helped to make the Assembly's influence more continuous, but it has been seriously hampered, particularly by the Soviet boycott. The Uniting for Peace resolution has reinforced the responsibility of the Assembly for meeting any aggression or menace to peace with which the Security Council shows itself indisposed to deal.

PROBLEMS FOR THE FUTURE

Among the most fundamental issues that emerge from the Assembly's development are the questions: how has this evolution affected the relationship between the Assembly and the Security Council and how desirable is this trend for the United Nations as a whole? We have seen above that this development has not actually endowed the Assembly with any powers not already implicit, if not explicit, in the Charter, nor has it displaced the Security Council. What it has done is to give the Assembly a stature in the political field that is more commensurate with that of the Council than was originally intended. To be more specific about the impact of this metamorphosis upon the Council, certain questions have been submitted directly to the Assembly which under different circumstances might have gone to the Security Council first. Furthermore the Assembly's increasing tendency to be active in the political field on a continuous basis allows it to deal with questions that arise between sessions which previously would probably have been referred to the Security Council. The Assembly has also used various devices to hitch its wagon to the Security Council's authority under Chapter VII: by issuing recommendations directly to the Council as in the Spanish and Palestine cases; by making recommendations to an agency established by the Council as in the case of the United Nations Command in Korea; and by making certain of its own agencies such as the Palestine Mediator responsible to the Council as well as the Assembly.

The Uniting for Peace resolution has also cast a heavy shadow across the Security Council by providing for the mobilization of military contingents on a voluntary basis in order to compensate for the Council's inability to call upon such forces through binding decisions. One may wonder of course whether the compulsory system anticipated in Article 43 of the Charter would ever have been implemented even without the present world conflict. The Assembly voluntary system is also likely to encounter difficulty in overcoming the reluctance on the part of most nations, small as well as large, to surrender or share control of their armed forces. This attude was conspicuous during the Fourth Meeting of Consultation of Foreign Ministers of American States held in Washington at the end of March 1951.

On the other hand most United Nations Members, including the United States, have made it clear that they do not want to abandon the Security Council altogether and are quite willing to allow it to operate when it is capable of doing so. It should not be forgotten that the Assembly has depended heavily on the Council to assist it in opposing aggressive intervention in both Palestine and Korea. It is also interesting to note that the Uniting for Peace resolution provides that only if and when "the Security Council, because of a lack of unanimity of the permanent members, fails to exercise its primary responsibility for the maintenance of international peace" is the General Assembly committed to "consider the matter immediately with a view to making appropriate recommendations to the Members for collective measures." The Peace Observation Commission may also receive orders from the Security Council, and the Collective Measures Committee is directed to make its report to the

Security Council as well as the Assembly. The military contingents and other resources which the Members are requested to make available to the United Nations are to be subject to recommendations by the Council as well as the Assembly. Thus the Council was woven into the whole fabric of the Uniting for Peace resolution.

This brief summary of the actual impact of the Assembly's development upon the Council serves as background for the important question: how desirable is this development in terms of the interests of the United Nations as a whole? The basic thesis of those who believe that the Security Council should play the leading role in the political field, with respect to pacific settlement as well as enforcement action, is that any political situation may eventually call for the use of force and that such enforcement measures cannot be successful unless they are unanimously supported by the great powers. In reply to this thesis one may say first that many decisions in the political field do not depend for their effectiveness upon the possible use of force. And even in the area of enforcement action unity among the great powers is desirable only to the extent that it helps to maintain peace with a minimum of political, economic and social justice. Few people would suggest that unity among the great powers is our most precious commodity to be purchased at any price — even allowing aggression to go unchecked because the great powers in the Security Council cannot agree among themselves. If carried to this extreme, great power unity may be more conducive to conflict than concord and may lead to the deterioration of the United Nations through dry rot. In the face of such a challenge it would seem preferable to have a little less unity in favor of a little more justice.

The experience of the past five years has demonstrated, moreover, that a lack of unity among the great powers does not necessarily render collective action ineffective as long as a preponderance of power can still be mobilized against an aggressor. Those who decry this development as a return to the wicked "balance of power" tradition forget that some balancing of power is part of every political organization. No international body can or should attempt to eliminate this balancing of forces altogether but should merely try to regulate the process and keep it within certain bounds. Because the present development of the Assembly's political role serves to keep the balancing process within the framework of the United Nations, rather than forcing it to operate outside, and because at the same time it allows the United Nations to avoid a complete deadlock due to the use of the veto in the Security Council, it would seem to be a development capable of strengthening rather than weakening the United Nations.

On the other hand in choosing the path that leads to the Assembly it is important to understand the risks that are involved. The greatest danger is that there is no guarantee that an Assembly resolution, although it is supported by at least two-thirds of the members, will have the backing of a sufficient number of influential states to make it effective. One must depend, therefore, upon the wisdom and self-discipline of the members themselves — qualities which fortunately have been demonstrated in most of the Assembly's major political decisions. Another danger is that as greater emphasis is placed on the use of force the Assembly may tend to neglect the more constructive non-military means of easing international tensions.

Some of the Assembly's partisans have urged that this organ be given greater authority in the political field because it is more "democratic" than the Security Council. This is a difficult argument to deal with since the word "democracy" has been pulled in so many different directions that it is stretched quite out of shape. Nevertheless perhaps one may say that the organization of an international assembly, like that of the usual national legislature, is democratic to the extent that it includes spokesmen of all elements in the community and gives them a voice roughly equivalent to their relative position within the total society. According to this yardstick the Assembly is obviously more representative than the Security Council in the sense that it includes spokesmen of a larger segment of the international community. It is not very representative, however, in assigning one vote to each state regardless of size, population or development. While there is no consensus as to the best means of weighting the votes of the members, there is a rather general recognition of the fact, for example, that the Soviet Union should be given more weight than El Salvador. Although various informal practices within the Assembly have tended to augment the influence of the weightier states, these nations will never really trust the Assembly until a more equitable arrangement is put into effect.

Aside from the voting question it has also been said that the Assembly's size and lack of continuity seriously limit its usefulness in the political field. While it is true that the Assembly's large membership makes it a more cumbersome body than the Security Council, the Assembly has done a great deal, as has every national legislature, to compensate for its size by establishing smaller and more flexible bodies to operate under its general direction. It is this proliferation of both sub-committees and field agencies which is one of the most significant aspects of the Assembly's development. By means of this experience the Assembly is gradually building the foundation for a truly responsible executive arm.

The Assembly has also recognized the need to achieve greater continuity of influence in the political field. The devices it has used for this purpose have included: a host of agencies which have dealt with specific problems on a continuing basis, the Interim Committee, the Peace Observation Commission, the provision in its Rules for convoking special sessions on twenty-four hour notice, and the extension of the fifth session beyond the usual period. The last is probably the most useful of these methods, but greater thought must still be given to this problem, particularly when dealing with fluid crisis situations, like Korea, which need unremitting supervision and direction.

Finally, the Assembly's experience with situations such as those in Palestine, Korea and the former Italian Colonies has demonstrated that each so-called "political" problem has within it issues which are usually thought of as "non-political" or "economic and social" and which are of crucial importance with regard to the total situation. In Libya there can be no stable independent government unless there is an adequate economic base to support it. In Korea there can be no long-range easing of tensions unless economic and social as well as political conditions are vastly improved. These considerations may well be cited as another reason why the Assembly should be the ultimate coordinator of policies regarding such situations rather than the Security Council which has no direct authority in the economic and social field. At the same time the Assembly's past experience suggests that it can and should do a great deal more in the future to bring to bear upon these problems its full constructive powers in the economic and social sphere.

The larger meaning of the Assembly's development in the political field during the past five years is that it reflects the realization by the great majority of United Nations Members that they are all interdependent rather than independent. They have begun to learn that one can scarcely cage political problems within the narrow confines of a council composed of only eleven of the United Nations' sixty Members. The effective formulation and implementation of practicable and just policies requires the regular collaboration of a far more extensive circle of influential countries. Greater pressure can be exerted within the larger body to iron away individual differences. Moreover, we have seen that the consideration of "political" issues cannot be separated from "non-political" economic and social issues; though these are matters of varying political intensities they are all part of the same spectrum.

Additional efforts must be made, however, to adjust the Assembly's structure and procedures to its increasing responsibilities. Its influence in the political field must be made continuous on a more effective basis; its organization, more flexible; its voting, more realistic. Some observers are saddened by the distance that still remains between the Assembly and the millennium of world government. They should be encouraged, however, by the present tendency to strengthen the hand of the most representative organ of the United Nations, which is a long step in the right direction. What is most significant is that the Assembly has proved itself during these trying five years to be an instrument sensitive to the needs of the great majority of nations and capable of remarkable development in order to achieve the purposes and principles espoused by that majority.

APPENDIX

MAJOR GENERAL ASSEMBLY RESOLUTIONS IN THE POLITICAL FIELD[1]

I. Specific Situations

China

Promotion of the stability of international relations in the Far East. (General Assembly Resolution 291 (IV).)

Threats to the political independence and territorial integrity of China and to the peace of the Far East, resulting from Soviet violations of the Sino-Soviet Treaty of Friendship and Alliance of 14 August 1945 and from Soviet violations of the Charter of the United Nations. (General Assembly Resolution 292 (IV).)

Threats to the political independence and territorial integrity of China and to the peace of the Far East, resulting from Soviet violations of the Sino-Soviet Treaty of Friendship and Alliance of 14 August 1945 and from Soviet violations of the Charter of the United Nations. (General Assembly Resolution 383 (V).)

Question of the representation of China in the General Assembly. (General Assembly Resolution 490 (V).)

Greece

Threats to the political independence and territorial integrity of Greece. (General Assembly Resolutions 109 (II); 193 (III); 288 (IV); 382 (V).)

Human Rights: Violations in Bulgaria, Hungary, Rumania

Observance in Bulgaria and Hungary of human rights and fundamental freedoms. (General Assembly Resolution 272 (III).)

---

1 NOTE: The sessions in which resolutions were adopted are indicated by the numerals in parentheses. The letter "S" denotes a special session.

Observance in Bulgaria, Hungary and Rumania of human rights and fundamental freedoms. (General Assembly Resolutions 294 (IV); 385 (V).)

Korea

The problem of the independence of Korea. (General Assembly Resolutions 112 (II); 195 (III); 293 (IV); 376 (V).)

Intervention of the Central People's Government of the People's Republic of China in Korea. (General Assembly Resolution 384 (V).)

Indians vs. South Africa

Treatment of Indians in the Union of South Africa. (General Assembly Resolution 44 (I).)

Treatment of people of Indian origin in the Union of South Africa. (General Assembly Resolutions 265 (III); 395 (V).)

Indonesia

Question of Indonesia. (General Assembly Resolutions 274 (III); 301 (IV).)

Italian Colonies: Libya, Somaliland, Eritrea

Problems of economic development and social progress of the former Italian colonies. (General Assembly Resolution 266 (III).)

Question of the disposal of the former Italian colonies. (General Assembly Resolutions 287 (III); 289 (IV).)

Libya: Report of the United Nations Commissioner in Libya; reports of the administering powers in Libya. (General Assembly Resolution 387 (V).)

Eritrea: Report of the United Nations Commission for Eritrea; report of the Interim Committee of the General Assembly on the report of the United Nations Commission for Eritrea. (General Assembly Resolution 390 (V).)

Non-Self-Governing Territories

Non-Self-Governing peoples. (General Assembly Resolution 9 (I).)

Transmission of information under Article 73e of the Charter. (General Assembly Resolution 66 (I).)

Regional Conferences of Representatives of Non-Self-Governing Territories. (General Assembly Resolution 67 (I).)

Standard form for the guidance of Members in the preparation of information to be transmitted under Article 73e of the Charter. (General Assembly Resolution 142 (II).)

Voluntary transmission of information regarding the development of self-governing institutions in the Non-Self-Governing Territories. (General Assembly Resolution 144 (II).)

Collaboration of the specialized agencies in regard to Article 73e of the Charter. (General Assembly Resolution 145 (II).)

Creation of a special committee on information transmitted under Article 73e of the Charter. (General Assembly Resolution 146 (II).)

Transmission of information under Article 73e of the Charter. (General Assembly Resolution 218 (III).)

Special Committee on Information transmitted under Article 73e of the Charter. (General Assembly Resolution 219 (III).)

Liaison between the Economic and Social Council and the Special Committee on Information transmitted under Article 73e of the Charter. (General Assembly Resolution 220 (III).)

Collaboration of the specialized agencies in regard to Article 73e of the Charter. (General Assembly Resolution 221 (III).)

Cessation of the transmission of information under Article 73e of the Charter. (General Assembly Resolution 222 (III).)

Voluntary transmission of information under part I of the Standard Form concerning Non-Self-Governing Territories. (General Assembly Resolution 327 (IV).)

Equal treatment in matters relating to education in Non-Self-Governing Territories. (General Assembly Resolution 328 (IV).)

Language of instruction in Non-Self-Governing Territories. (General Assembly Resolution 329 (IV).)

Eradication of illiteracy in Non-Self-Governing Territories. (General Assembly Resolution 330 (IV).)

International collaboration in regard to economic, social and educational conditions in Non-Self-Governing Territories. (General Assembly Resolution 331 (IV).)

Establishment of a Special Committee on Information transmitted under Article 73e of the Charter. (General Assembly Resolution 332 (IV).)

Work of the Special Committee on Information transmitted under Article 73e of the Charter. (General Assembly Resolution 333 (IV).)

Territories to which Chapter XI of the Charter applies. (General Assembly Resolution 334 (IV).)

Technical assistance to Non-Self-Governing Territories. (General Assembly Resolution 444 (V).)

Work of the Special Committee on Information transmitted under Article 73e of the Charter. (General Assembly Resolution 445 (V).)

Palestine

Special Committee on Palestine. (General Assembly Resolution 106 (S-1).)

Future government of Palestine. (General Assembly Resolution 181 (II) .)

Protection of the city of Jerusalem and its inhabitants: reference to the Trusteeship Council. (General Assembly Resolution 185 (S-2).)

Appointment and terms of reference of a United Nations Mediator in Palestine. (General Assembly Resolution 186 (S-2).)

Protection of the city of Jerusalem and its inhabitants: appointment of a Special Municipal Commissioner. (General Assembly Resolution 187 (S-2).)

Appreciation of the work of the United Nations Palestine Commission. (General Assembly Resolution 189 (S-2).)

Palestine — Progress report of the United Nations Mediator. (General Assembly Resolution 194 (III).)

Assistance to Palestine refugees. (General Assembly Resolution 302 (IV).)

Palestine: question of an international regime for the Jerusalem area and the protection of the Holy Places. (General Assembly Resolution 303 (IV).)

Assistance to Palestine refugees. (General Assembly Resolution 393 (V) .)

Palestine: progress report of the United Nations Conciliation Commission for Palestine; repatriation or resettlement of Palestine refugees and payment of compensation due them. (General Assembly Resolution 394 (V).)

Spain

Relations of Members of the United Nations with Spain. (General Assembly Resolutions 32 (I); 39 (I); 114 (II).)
Relations of States Members and specialized agencies with Spain. (General Assembly Resolution 386 (V).)

Trusteeship

Approval of Trusteeship Agreements. (General Assembly Resolution 63 (I).)
Establishment of the Trusteeship Council. (General Assembly Resolution 64 (I).)
Future status of South West Africa. (General Assembly Resolution 65 (I).)
Report of the Trusteeship Council covering its first session. (General Assembly Resolution 139 (II).)
Proposed Trusteeship Agreement for Nauru. (General Assembly Resolution 140 (II).)
Consideration of proposed new trusteeship agreements, if any: question of South West Africa. (General Assembly Resolution 141 (II).)
Report of the Trusteeship Council covering its second and third sessions. (General Assembly Resolution 223 (III).)
Administrative unions affecting Trust Territories. (General Assembly Resolution 224 (III).)
Educational advancement in Trust Territories. (General Assembly Resolution 225 (III).)
Progressive development of Trust Territories. (General Assembly Resolution 226 (III).)
Question of South West Africa. (General Assembly Resolution 227 (III).)
Political advancement of Trust Territories. (General Assembly Resolution 320 (IV).)

Economic advancement in Trust Territories. (General Assembly Resolution 322 (IV).)

Social advancement in Trust Territories. (General Assembly Resolution 323 (IV).)

Educational advancement in Trust Territories. (General Assembly Resolution 324 (IV).)

Administrative unions affecting Trust Territories. (General Assembly Resolution 326 (IV).)

Question of South West Africa: reiteration of previous resolutions and submission of reports. (General Assembly Resolution 337 (IV).)

Question of South West Africa: request for an advisory opinion of the International Court of Justice. (General Assembly Resolution 338 (IV).)

Educational advancement in Trust Territories. (General Assembly Resolution 437 (V).)

Rural economic development of the Trust Territories. (General Assembly Resolution 438 (V).)

Technical assistance for Trust Territories. (General Assembly Resolution 439 (V).)

Trusteeship Agreement for the Territory of Somaliland under Italian administration. (General Assembly Resolution 442 (V).)

Administrative unions affecting Trust Territories. (General Assembly Resolution 443 (V).)

Question of South West Africa. (General Assembly Resolution 449 (V).)

II. GENERAL ISSUES

Armaments

Establishment of a Commission to deal with the Problems raised by the discovery of atomic energy. (General Assembly Resolution 1 (I).)

Principles governing the general regulation and reduction of armaments. (General Assembly Resolution 41 (I).)

Information on armed forces to be supplied by Members of the United Nations. (General Assembly Resolution 42 (I).)

Reports of the Atomic Energy Commission. (General Assembly Resolution 191 (III).)

Prohibition of the atomic weapon and reduction by one-third of the armaments and armed forces of the permanent members of the Security Council. (General Assembly Resolution 192 (III).)

International control of atomic energy. (General Assembly Resolution 299 (IV).)

Regulation and reduction of conventional armaments and armed forces. (General Assembly Resolution 300 (IV).)

International control of atomic energy. (General Assembly Resolution 496 (V).)

Development of International Law

Draft Declaration on the Rights and Duties of States. (General Assembly Resolution 38 (I).)

Draft Declaration on Fundamental Human Rights and Freedoms. (General Assembly Resolution 43 (I).)

Progressive development of International Law and its codification. (General Assembly Resolution 94 (I).)

Affirmation of the principles of International Law recognized by the Charter of the Nürnberg Tribunal. (General Assembly Resolution 95 (I).)

The crime of Genocide. (General Assembly Resolution 96 (I).)

Need for greater use by the United Nations and its organs of the International Court of Justice. (General Assembly Resolution 171 (II).)

Establishment of an International Law Commission. (General Assembly Resolution 174 (II).)

Formulation of the principles recognized in the Charter of the Nürnberg Tribunal and in the judgment of the Tribunal. (General Assembly Resolution 177 (II).)

Draft declaration on the rights and duties of States. (General Assembly Resolution 178 (II).)

Draft convention on genocide. (General Assembly Resolution 180 (II).)

Prevention and punishment of the crime of genocide. (General Assembly Resolution 260 (III).)

Invitations to be addressed to non-member States to become parties to the Convention on the Prevention and Punishment of the Crime of Genocide. (General Assembly Resolution 368 (IV).)

Approval of part I of the report of the International Law Commission covering its first session. (General Assembly 373 (IV).)

Recommendation to the International Law Commission to include the regime of territorial waters in its list of topics to be given priority. (General Assembly Resolution 374 (IV).)

Draft Declaration on rights and duties of States. (General Assembly Resolution (375 (IV).)

Ways and means for making the evidence of customary international law more readily available. (General Assembly Resolution 487 (V).)

Peace Proposals

Threat or use of force. (General Assembly Resolution 107 (S-1).)

Measures to be taken against propaganda and the inciters of a new war. (General Assembly Resolution 110 (II).)

Appeal to the great powers to renew their efforts to compose their differences and establish a lasting peace. (General Assembly Resolution 190 (III).)

Essentials of peace. (General Assembly Resolution 290 (IV).)

Peace through deeds. (General Assembly Resolution 380 (V).)

Condemnation of propaganda against peace. (General Assembly Resolution 381 (V).)

Development of a 20-year program for achieving peace through the United Nations. (General Assembly Resolution 494 (V).)

III. Organizational Issues

Admission to Membership

Admission of Afghanistan, Iceland and Sweden to membership in the United Nations. (General Assembly Resolution 34 (I).)

Question of the re-examination by the Security Council of certain applications for admission to membership in the United Nations. (General Assembly Resolution 35 (I).)

Rules governing the admission of new Members to the United Nations. (General Assembly Resolution 36 (I).)

Admission of Siam to membership in the United Nations. (General Assembly Resolution 101 (I).)

Admission of Yemen and Pakistan to membership in the United Nations. (General Assembly Resolution 108 (II).)

Admission of new Members. (General Assembly Resolution 113 (II).)

Rules governing the admission of new Members. (General Assembly Resolution 116 (II).)

Admission of the Union of Burma to membership in the United Nations. (General Assembly Resolution 188 (S-2).)

Admission of new Members. (General Assembly Resolution 197 (III).)

Admission of Israel to membership in the United Nations. (General Assembly Resolution 273 (III).)

Admission of new Members. (General Assembly Resolution 296 (IV).)

Admission of the Republic of Indonesia to membership in the United Nations. (General Assembly Resolution 491 (V).)

Admission of new Members to the United Nations. (General Assembly Resolution 495 (V).)

Assembly Methods and Procedures

Part III of the report of the Committee on Procedures and Organization of the General Assembly. (General Assembly Resolution 173 (II).)

Amendments to the rules of procedure of the General Assembly. (General Assembly Resolution 262 (III).)

Appointment of a Special Committee on Methods and Procedure of the General Assembly. (General Assembly Resolution 271 (III).)

Methods and procedures of the General Assembly. (General Assembly Resolution 362 (IV).)

Majority required for the adoption by the General Assembly of amendments to and parts of proposals relating to important questions. (General Assembly Resolution 475 (V).)

Interim Committee

Establishment of an Interim Committee of the General Assembly. (General Assembly Resolution 111 (II).)

Re-establishment of the Interim Committee of the General Assembly. (General Assembly Resolutions 196 (III); 295 (IV).)

International Cooperation in Political Field

Study of methods for the promotion of international cooperation in the political field. (General Assembly Resolution 268 (III).)

Duties of States in the event of the outbreak of hostilities. (General Assembly Resolution 378 (V).)

Establishment of a permanent Commission of Good Offices. (General Assembly Resolution 379 (V).)

Recognition in the United Nations

Recognition by the United Nations of the representation of a Member state. (General Assembly 396 (V).)

Uniting for Peace

Uniting for peace. (General Assembly Resolution 377 (V).)

United Nations Field Service and Panel of Field Observers

United Nations Guard. (General Assembly Resolution 270 (III).)

United Nations Field Service and United Nations Panel of Field Observers. (General Assembly Resolution 297 (IV).)

Voting in the Security Council

Voting procedure in the Security Council. (General Assembly Resolution 40 (I).)

Convocation of a general conference under Article 109 of the Charter to amend the privilege of the veto and resolution of the second part of the first session of the General Assembly in relation to the exercise of the veto. (General Assembly Resolution 117 (II).)

The problem of voting in the Security Council. (General Assembly Resolution 267 (III).)